MW01055099

{THE JOHN WALVOORD PROPHECY COMMENTARIES}

1 & 2
Thessalonians

John F. Walvoord and Mark Hitchcock

Edited by

Philip E. Rawley

MOODY PUBLISHERS
CHICAGO

© 2012 by
JOHN F. WALVOORD

Edited by Roy B. Zuck
Interior design: Ragont Design
Cover design: Tan Nguyen
Cover image: iStock photo

Library of Congress Cataloging-in-Publication Data

Walvoord, John F.
    1 & 2 Thessalonians / John F. Walvoord and Mark Hitchcock ; edited by
Philip E. Rawley.
        p. cm. — (The John Walvoord prophecy commentaries)
    Includes bibliographical references (p.   ) and indexes.
    ISBN 978-0-8024-0248-6
    1. Bible. N.T. Thessalonians—Commentaries. I. Hitchcock, Mark, 1959-
II. Rawley, Philip E. III. Title. IV. Title: 1 and 2 Thessalonians.
BS2725.53.W35 2012
227'.8107—dc23

                                                        2011047251

We hope you enjoy this book from Moody Publishers. Our goal is to provide high-quality, thought-provoking books and products that connect truth to your real needs and challenges. For more information on other books and products written and produced from a biblical perspective, go to www.moodypublishers.com or write to:

Moody Publishers
820 N. LaSalle Boulevard
Chicago, IL 60610

3 5 7 9 10 8 6 4 2

Printed in the United States of America

To my daughter-in-law, Natalee,
the best a father-in-law ever had.

You bring inexpressible love and
joy to my life and to our family.

—Mark Hitchcock

Dr. Mark Hitchcock graduated from law school in 1984 and worked for a judge at the Oklahoma Court of Criminal Appeals. After a clear call to full-time ministry, Mark attended Dallas Theological Seminary, graduating in 1991. Since that time he has served as senior pastor of Faith Bible Church in Edmond, Oklahoma. He completed his PhD at Dallas Theological Seminary in 2005 and serves as an adjunct faculty member at DTS in the Bible Exposition Department. He has authored over twenty books related to end-times Bible prophecy.

Philip E. Rawley is a former Moody Publishers textbook editor, one of the founding editors and writers for *Today in the Word*, and a freelance writer living in Rockwall, Texas. He is a graduate of the University of South Florida (BA) and Dallas Theological Seminary (ThM). Phil and his wife, Sarah, have two children and a grandson.

Contents

Foreword

In the last few weeks before my father died we had time to celebrate his life, tell stories about past family events, and dream a little about the future. His mind and memory were sharp and he was as upbeat and confident as ever. He was ninety-two years of age, had lived a full life, and had served well the Lord he loved.

The doctors had given him six weeks to live, and in that time we relived many a family story. He was visited by a parade of his close friends, many influential leaders he had taught and mentored. From his hospital room were days filled with warm memories and laughter, and an occasional hymn echoed down the hall.

My father had a list of things he entrusted to me as his oldest son. But in the last week of his life, the conversation turned to the seventy years he had dedicated to the study of the Bible. And in all that time, he explained, four key books of the Bible had been the subject of his most intense study; *Revelation, Daniel, Matthew,* and *1st and 2nd Thessalonians.* He shared stories about how they were first written, taught, and eventually published.

I remember many of those times. Every summer our family piled into our car and drove across the U.S. and sometimes into Canada. We went from one Bible conference to another, but a lot of that time was spent on the road. And always somewhere in the car was a cardboard box filled with books.

Many nights Dad put us to bed and quietly went into a motel bathroom to read and take notes. Then when he was ready he would dictate an entire chapter, footnotes and all. So whether on the road or at home, this scholarly work was often done late at night and early in the morning. And it continued all his life.

His dream in those final conversations was that his work and biblical insights would live on after him. He remembered how the commentaries and works of some of the great teachers of the Bible lived on for generation after generation. Would his commentaries survive to teach others after his death?

My father explained he had chosen Moody Publishers (then known as Moody Press) to publish his first commentary on *Revelation* for one very important reason. He knew he could trust them to keep the commentary in print as long as it was needed.

So in those last weeks of my father's life, our discussions produced one more assignment. Could I find a way to fulfill his dream to keep these works alive for the generations of students he would not be able to teach in the classroom?

From the seed of that dream has grown the new Walvoord Commentary series. The team that took up that dream is made up of men my father knew and trusted. And as he would have guessed, it was championed by Greg Thornton, senior vice president of Moody Publishers.

Philip Rawley agreed to take the lead as the editor of the series. And he took on the assignment with much more than the word "editor" implies. Phil was both a student of my father's and a friend. As far back as twenty-five years ago he collaborated with me to help my father with a project that became *Every Prophecy of the Bible*. Since then we have worked together on many writing projects.

But I believe this may have been one of Phil Rawley's most important tasks. He was much more than an editor. In many instances he took up the mantle of the writer who could best capture the way my father would have explained his biblical insights to a new generation of students.

Dr. Mark Hitchcock also agreed to join the team. Because of Mark's interest in prophecy, he and my father often had lunch to discuss key issues in biblical prophecy. Mark is a great admirer of my father's work and a prolific author in his own right who had written more than fifteen books on prophecy and end-time events before we met. Mark was a natural choice to work with me to research and write *Armageddon, Oil, and Terror* shortly after my father's death. In that process we became close friends in the quest to turn my father's ideas and notes into an entirely new work. It was an amazing journey.

Dr. Hitchcock has collaborated on *Revelation* and has taken on the lion's share of expanding my father's work and class notes, previously published as *The Thessalonian Epistles*, into a full commentary for this series. He is a thorough scholar who fully understands my father's teaching from the Epistles.

Dr. Charles Dyer also became an important part of the team. He is an author and teacher who has been greatly influenced by my father as one of his students and later a colleague in the administration of Dallas Theological Seminary. As an Old Testament scholar, Dr. Dyer has taken up the task of revising my father's commentary on *Daniel*, and has also agreed to work on *Matthew's Gospel* for two reasons. First, most of Jesus' teaching on prophecy is best understood in its Old Testament context. Second, Dr. Dyer is as familiar with the Holy Land and the setting of Matthew as anyone I know. He will, I am sure, make both Daniel and the events of *Matthew's Gospel* come alive for every reader of the Walvoord Commentary series.

So now, almost a decade after my father's death, his legacy will live on in this new series of biblical commentaries. I am sure he would have been proud of the men who have taken up his torch and are passing it to a new generation of Bible students. As a great man of "The Book," my father is greater still because those who follow in his footsteps remain true to his vision and faithful to the exposition of God's Word.

John Edward Walvoord
January 2011

8

Preface

The first time I met Dr. Walvoord was as a child when he would come regularly to speak at the church I attended. I will never forget the first time, when as a teenager, I got the nerve to go up front after a sermon to ask him a prophecy question. He was very tall, very imposing, and very matter-of-fact, yet there was a kindness and a smile that shone through. Thus, without either of us knowing at the time, a relationship was begun that would last until his death in 2002 and beyond.

When I attended Dallas Theological Seminary, Dr. Walvoord had retired as President and was serving as Chancellor. I had a strong interest in Bible prophecy, so I sought out Dr. Walvoord to soak up everything I could from him. At first, we would sit in his office, but later, when he realized that I was serious about learning all I could, we began to have lunch together regularly at the Dixie House restaurant in Dallas. He would always drive while I asked questions. Later, while I was working on my doctorate, I was in Dallas less frequently, but we still met together for lunch many times. We would discuss eschatology, but as our relationship deepened he would also tell me stories about his life and ministry and God's leading. I drank in every drop. Those times with him are some of my fondest memories.

After Dr. Walvoord went to be with the Lord in 2002, I began to think about the possibility of updating and revising some of his work. I prayed about what to do and decided to call his son Dr. John E. Walvoord, whom I had never met. As John and I talked there was an instant connection. We both loved his father; we both loved prophecy; and we both wanted to see his legacy extended. The first book we worked on together was Dr. Walvoord's classic *Armageddon, Oil and the Middle East Crisis*. During our work on that book my love and respect for John grew. We shared some great times together reminiscing about his father, brainstorming, writing, and rewriting. After finishing that project, John decided to undertake the challenge of revising his father's commentaries on Revelation, Daniel, the Thessalonian epistles, and Matthew, and with the help of Moody Publishers this current series was born.

I was privileged to work with Philip Rawley on the Revelation revision, and he also edited this present work. He has become a beloved coworker and friend. He is very skilled at what he does, and I have learned a great deal from him. Phil would also like to thank Bethany, his daughter and assistant, for her invaluable help on this commentary.

Working on this series is one of the great joys and honors of my life. I loved Dr. Walvoord, and I hope he would be pleased with our meager efforts to keep his legacy alive. But most of all, I hope our Lord is pleased because that is what Dr. Walvoord would have wanted above all else.

Mark Hitchcock
Edmond, Oklahoma
June 3, 2011

Introduction

BACKGROUND

Thessalonica was founded in 315 B.C. by Cassander, who was one of Alexander the Great's generals. Cassander named the city after his wife Thessaloniki, who was Alexander's stepsister. Like Esther and Ruth in the Old Testament, the Thessalonian epistles trace their name to a famous woman.

Thessalonica is situated on the Thermaic Gulf and is an important port city in Macedonia. The modern city of Salonica or Thessaloniki is Greece's second-largest city. In the first century Thessalonica was the capital of Macedonia and a thriving commercial center with a population of about 200,000. The city was also strategically situated on the *Via Egnatia*, or Egnatian Way, a major stone highway that was an extension of the Appian Way in Italy and connected Rome to the East.

AUTHORSHIP AND OCCASION
OF 1 THESSALONIANS

The church of Thessalonica was founded by Paul and Silas on Paul's second missionary journey in the spring of A.D. 50. After their imprisonment and release in Philippi, Paul and Silas traveled along the Egnatian Way about one hundred miles to the next major city, Thessalonica. Luke and Timothy were left behind in Philippi to establish the infant church there. Timothy later rejoined Paul and Silas in Berea (Acts 17:10–14).

When the apostle Paul, accompanied by Silas, entered Thessalonica, their ministry was probably the first gospel witness ever given there. Acts 17:1–9 records the amazing results of their ministry.

Now when they had passed through Amphipolis and Apollonia, they came to Thessalonica, where there was a synagogue of the Jews. And Paul went in, as was his custom, and on three Sabbath days he reasoned with them from the Scriptures, explaining and proving that it was necessary for the Christ to suffer and to rise from the dead, and saying, "This Jesus, whom I proclaim to you, is the Christ." And some of them were persuaded and joined Paul and Silas, as did a great many of the devout Greeks and not a few of the leading women. But the Jews were jealous, and taking some wicked men of the rabble, they formed a mob, set the city in an uproar, and attacked the house of Jason, seeking to bring them out to the crowd. And when they could not find them, they dragged Jason and some of the brothers before the city authorities, shouting, "These men who have turned the world upside down have come here also, and Jason has received them, and they are all acting against the decrees of Caesar, saying that there is another king, Jesus." And the people and the city authorities were disturbed when they heard these things. And when they had taken money as security from Jason and the rest, they let them go.

These verses show the thrust of Paul's message as he spent those three Sabbaths reasoning with the people. He emphasized three key points: (1) The Messiah of the Old Testament had to suffer and rise again from the dead (Acts 17:3); (2) Jesus is the promised Messiah (Acts 17:3); and (3) Jesus is the King who will return to earth to reign (Acts 17:7). In a few short weeks, a small group of Thessalonians came to know Jesus Christ as their Savior.

Because of Paul's success, the Jews were moved with jealousy and gathered a group of worthless thugs from the marketplace to set the city in an uproar. When they discovered that Paul and Silas were at the home of Jason, they dragged Jason and some of the other believers before the ruling body (*politarchs*) of the city. The rulers made Jason and the others post a bond and released them. The bond may have included some assurance that Paul and Silas would leave town and not return (cf. 1 Thess. 2:18). Paul and Silas left the city that night, realizing that their presence was causing added affliction for the believers. Their next stop was fifty miles south on the Egnatian Way in Berea (Acts 17:10). Once again they encountered opposition when some antagonistic Jews from Thessalonica heard about Paul's preaching, came to Berea, and incited the people to run Paul out of their city.

After leaving Berea, Paul traveled alone to Athens (Acts 17:16–34), and then on to Corinth. He was deeply concerned about the plight of the new believers in Thessalonica, so he sent Timothy there to check on their welfare. Some months later Timothy and Silas rejoined Paul in Corinth, bringing him news of conditions in the Thessalonian church (Acts 18:5; 1 Thess. 3:1–6). From this series of events we can reconstruct the background of the epistle:

1. Paul, Silas, Timothy, and Luke came to Philippi.
2. Paul and Silas went on to Thessalonica, leaving Timothy and Luke in Philippi (Acts 17:4, 10).
3. Timothy left Philippi to rejoin Paul and Silas in Berea (Acts 17:14).
4. Paul departed from Berea, leaving Silas and Timothy there with instructions to join him in Athens (Acts 17:14–15).
5. Silas and Timothy rejoined Paul at Athens (Acts 17:16).
6. Timothy was sent to Thessalonica from Athens (1 Thess. 3:2). Since Timothy was not with Paul and Silas when they were forced out of town, he could visit the city without forfeiting the bond that was posted by Jason and the others (Acts 17:9).
7. After Timothy left, Silas was also sent to Thessalonica (Acts 18:5).
8. Paul traveled from Athens to Corinth (Acts 18:1).
9. Timothy and Silas came to Paul at Corinth from Macedonia at the same time (Acts 18:5; 1 Thess. 3:6).
10. After hearing of the continued faithfulness of the Thessalonian converts to Christ in the midst of persecution, Paul sent them the communication known to us as his first epistle to the Thessalonians in A.D. 50 or 51 from Corinth. He sent the letter in his name and those of Silas and Timothy (1 Thess. 1:1) to give the Thessalonians encouragement and remind them of his love and faithful prayer for them.

One of the central questions related to the Thessalonian letters is the length of Paul's original stay in the city. Based on Acts 17:2, Paul was in Thessalonica for at least three Sabbath days. Many maintain that this was the full length of Paul's time in Thessalonica. However, it seems that he was there for a longer period, probably two or three months. Four points favor this longer stay:

1. Paul received at least two financial gifts from Philippi while one hundred miles away in Thessalonica (Phil. 4:16). This would seem to require more than three weeks.
2. Paul settled down long enough in Thessalonica to pursue his secular trade (1 Thess. 2:9; 2 Thess. 3:7–10).
3. Paul's familiarity with the people and the extent of his pastoral care indicate a longer stay (1 Thess. 2:7–8).
4. First Thessalonians contains no direct Old Testament quotations and only one Old Testament allusion, in 5:1–3. This indicates that a majority of the church members were Gentiles. Paul must have had a ministry to Gentiles between Acts 17:4 and 5. This would fit with what we know of Paul's normal pattern in other locations of going to the Jew first and then turning to the Gentiles (Acts 13:46; 18:6; 19:8–9). A three-week ministry to Jews would not have allowed Paul enough time to minister to the city's Gentiles, who were evidently the primary recipients of 1 Thessalonians.

While some maintain that Paul was in Thessalonica for three to six months, a visit of two to three months fits all the facts well. Either way, this was still a very short time for Paul to communicate so much truth to this group of young believers.

THEME OF 1 THESSALONIANS

First Thessalonians is of special interest to believers in Christ today for a number of reasons. First, this epistle is considered by many to be the first inspired letter written by Paul. While this is possible, it is more likely that Galatians was the first letter and 1 Thessalonians was the second. But whether the first, or one of the earliest, letters addressed to young Christians, it is a significant example of the rich doctrinal and practical content of Pauline teaching.

Second, in every chapter the theme of the return of the Lord is prominent. For this reason, 1 and 2 Thessalonians together have often been called Paul's "eschatological epistles." In 1 Thessalonians, 23 of 89 verses relate to the future. This represents about 26 percent of the book. Second Thessalonians is even more heavily weighted toward the end times, with 19 of its 47 verses dealing with the future. That is 40 percent of its content.[1]

First Thessalonians unfolds around the prominent theme of the Lord's coming. The first chapter unpacks the great theme of the Lord's coming in relation to *salvation*. In chapter 2, the Lord's coming in relation to Christian *service* is presented. Chapter 3 relates *sanctification* to the Lord's coming. In chapter 4 the Lord's coming is revealed as the *surety* of resurrection of our loved ones who have died in Christ. Chapter 5, which concludes the epistle, deals with the *safety* of the believer in the days of the wrath of God preceding the second coming of Christ. Throughout the epistle the theme of the coming of the Lord is related to practical Christian living.

Third, the richness of Paul's teaching is evident in a study of 1 Thessalonians. Speaking of both 1 and 2 Thessalonians Charles Ryrie says, "The Epistles are like finely cut gems. They reflect the depths of theological thought, especially in the area of future things; they mirror the pattern of teaching which the apostle used with new Gentile converts; from every part shine forth the character and conduct of Paul's missionary heart; they sparkle with the brilliance of the captivating power of the gospel of the grace of Christ."[2] Though the Thessalonians were young Christians with less than a year of Christian experience, nevertheless they were familiar with the great and deep truths of the Christian faith, such as salvation, election, sanctification, assurance, the Trinity, the nature of humanity, resurrection, and the day of the Lord.

It is hard to realize as one reads 1 Thessalonians that the Christians to whom it was addressed had no New Testament. It is also doubtful that they had any large portion of the Old Testament. They were immature Christians, with many trials and difficulties, and enduring much persecution. In the midst of their tribulations some of their number had gone on to be with the Lord, and with this in view Paul wrote them this letter of comfort, exhortation, and instruction.

PURPOSE OF 1 THESSALONIANS

When studying any biblical book, it is helpful to consider the purpose of the book, to ask, Why was this book written to the original audience? The content of 1 Thessalonians suggests that the apostle Paul wrote this letter with three key purposes in mind.

1. To express his thanks to God for them (1:2; 2:13; 3:9)
2. To explain why he had not yet visited them again (2:17–18)
3. To correct doctrinal (3:10; 4:13; 5:1–11) and practical (4:1–12; 5:12–18) problems.

OUTLINE OF 1 THESSALONIANS

I. The Coming of the Lord and Salvation (1:1–10)
II. The Coming of the Lord and Service (2:1–20)
III. The Coming of the Lord and Sanctification (3:1–13)
IV. The Coming of the Lord and Surety (4:1–18)
V. The Coming of the Lord and Safety (5:1–28)

CONTRASTS BETWEEN 1 AND 2 THESSALONIANS

1 THESSALONIANS	2 THESSALONIANS
Emphasis on the coming of the Lord in the air *for* His saints	Emphasis on the coming of the Lord to the earth *with* His saints
Coming of Christ	Coming of Antichrist
Theme is comfort	Theme is correction

AUTHORSHIP AND OCCASION
OF 2 THESSALONIANS

While still at Corinth, shortly after writing 1 Thessalonians, Paul received more news about the condition of the church at Thessalonica. With Silas and Timothy at his side, Paul wrote this second letter to the church probably about two or three months after 1 Thessalonians.

The occasion for 2 Thessalonians was the receipt of the news that the Thessalonians had received a spurious letter, apparently an intentional forgery, teaching them that they were already in the day of the Lord and its awful judgments. The background of both Thessalonian epistles indicates that the church was going through a terrible time of persecution and hardship. In the midst of these trials, they began to wonder if they were in the day of the Lord, a period described at great length in the Old Testament and concerning which Paul had taught them, both when he was with them and in writing 1 Thessalonians 5.

The beginning of this period of tremendous trouble and conflict in the world is identified with the great judgments that will be poured out on the world before the second coming of Christ. The Thessalonians, on the basis of the forged letter, wondered if they were in this time of trouble, in contradiction to Paul's teaching that the church would be translated before the day of the Lord began (1 Thess. 4:13–5:9). Paul penned this letter to correct this misunderstanding. Paul's answer, in a word, was that this predicted time of trouble which begins the day of the Lord was still future. The persecutions they were undergoing were the normal persecutions that may be experienced by all Christians throughout the church age.

PURPOSE OF 2 THESSALONIANS

The primary purpose for this epistle was to correct a wrong understanding concerning the day of the Lord. Some false teachers had produced spurious information to the effect that Paul had said the day of the Lord was present (2:1). Since the church at Thessalonica was undergoing severe persecution, this appeared to be a logical conclusion (1 Thess. 1:6; 2:14; 3:3). The second purpose was to comfort and encourage the Thessalonian believers to remain steadfast under persecution (1:4–12). A third purpose was to correct disorderliness in the church. Some believed they could leave their jobs because the coming of the Lord was so near (3:6–16).

OUTLINE OF 2 THESSALONIANS

I. Introduction (1:1–2)
II. A Word of Comfort (1:3–12)
    Pastoral   The Revelation of Christ
III. A Word of Caution (2:1–17)
    Prophetic   The Rebellion of Antichrist
IV. A Word of Command (3:1–16)
    Practical   The Responsibility of Christians
V. Conclusion (3:17–18)

Three main groups of people are addressed in this epistle: (1) Persecutors of the church (chapter 1); (2) False teachers (chapter 2); and (3) Idle church members (chapter 3). Also, each chapter ends with a prayer: (1) prayer for power (1:11–12); (2) prayer for comfort and strength (2:16–17); and (3) prayer for peace (3:16–17).

NOTES

1. Richard Mayhue, *First and Second Thessalonians: Triumphs and Trials of a Consecrated Church* (Fearn, Ross-shire, Scotland: Christian Focus, 1999), 45. The *Tim LaHaye Study Bible* computes that 18 percent of 1 Thessalonians (16 of 89 verses) is prophetic, but agrees that 40 percent (19 of 47 verses) of 2 Thessalonians is prophecy (Tim LaHaye, gen. ed., *Tim LaHaye Prophecy Study Bible* [Chattanooga, TN: AMG, 2001], 1406, 1413).
2. Charles Caldwell Ryrie, *First and Second Thessalonians,* Everyman's Bible Commentary (Chicago: Moody, 1959), 7.

1

Salvation in Relation to the Coming of the Lord
1 Thessalonians 1:1–10

OPENING SALUTATION (1:1)

1:1 Paul, Silvanus, and Timothy, to the church of the Thessalonians in God the Father and the Lord Jesus Christ: Grace to you and peace.

Chapter 1 opens with a very simple salutation: "Paul, Silvanus, and Timothy, to the church of the Thessalonians." Noteworthy here is the fact that as in 2 Thessalonians 2:1, no apostolic titles are mentioned. Only the names Paul, and Silvanus—which was another name for Silas—and Timothy were listed. Paul and Silas had brought the gospel to the Thessalonians on the apostles' second missionary journey (Acts 17:1–9); later Timothy made a trip from Athens back to Thessalonica and reported to Paul what he had discovered (1 Thess. 3:1–6). The report was an epic of the steadfastness and faithfulness of the Thessalonian Christians. He told Paul that in spite of persecution the Thessalonians had a good testimony for Jesus Christ and were faithfully sharing the gospel message.

The first verse of this book includes a contrast between the position the believers had in Christ and their current *state* of persecution and uncertainty (1:6). Paul addressed them as "the church of the Thessalonians" which is "in God the Father and the Lord Jesus Christ." Nothing could change their position, which included everything that was theirs because of being in Christ. They remained true no matter what happened. This young, persecuted church needed above all else to know that they were in God the Father and Jesus Christ. But they needed more than this knowledge.

Paul prayed for them with two words that would become trademarks in his later epistles: "Grace to you, and peace." How rich are the simple words "grace" and "peace." Those without grace and peace are in utter poverty though they may possess all the riches of the world. Those with grace and peace are infinitely rich, though enduring persecution and sorrow as did the Thessalonians. Grace expressed the whole of God's love and favor in Christ. Peace *with* God (salvation) and the peace *of* God (the daily assurance of His presence and care) are priceless possessions of the child of God. What richer jewels from God's treasures could be asked for than these? While in a sense the Thessalonians already had God's grace and peace, they needed its manifestation, its experience, its triumph.

A BURST OF PRAISE (1:2–3)

1:2 We give thanks to God always for all of you, constantly mentioning you in our prayers.

The apostle began with praise to God for the believers at Thessalonica. This is more or less the theme of the whole epistle—his thankfulness to God for saving these Thessalonians through their faith in Christ. He breathed out this prayer from his very heart in verse 2. Verses 2–10 are one long sentence in Greek, with "give thanks" as the main verb. This entire sentence highlights all that Paul gave thanks for in the lives of these faithful believers. The emphasis was not on buildings, facilities, organization, structure, staff, curriculum, or budget. Not that these things do not matter, or that they cannot greatly help us. They are needed, but they are not the key. The focus here is on people. Paul gave thanks for the spiritual qualities of these believers.

Again something of the faithfulness of Paul's prayer ministry is indicated in the phrase, "We give thanks to God always." In the days and months that had passed since he left this little band of believers in Thessalonica whom he loved, Paul had been faithful in prayer for them. What a rebuke it is to many of us who serve the Lord that often our hearts are not burdened with the needs of God's people. Nor are we thankful for the Lord's grace in their lives, especially when they are out of sight and out of mind. But Paul gave his testimony: "We give thanks to God always for all of you." Of interest is the fact that Paul did not thank the Thessalonians; he thanked God.

This expression "for all of you" or "for you all" is significant. "You all" is used in the southern United States as an expansive, general expression referring to one person or many. Paul, however, used it very accurately here. He was thanking God for *all* of them. In each life and heart the Spirit of God had done His work in such a way that souls had been saved and were now bearing a faithful testimony for the Lord Jesus Christ. As we consider our own lives and testimony, do our pastors and Sunday school teachers—those with whom we work in Christian service—thank God for us *always*? Certainly there is a challenge to us here to be like the Thessalonians and so to live before God and our fellow Christians that they may thank God always for us.

1:3 Remembering before our God and Father your work of faith and labor of love and steadfastness of hope in our Lord Jesus Christ.

As Paul prayed for the Thessalonians, he thanked God for some of the great realities that comprise the salvation of the believer. The remaining verses of chapter 1 constitute a simple outline. First, in verse 3, Paul remembered what God had done through them and in them. Second, in verses 4–9, on the basis of what God had done, Paul knew certain things. Third, in verse 10 he expressed the hope of Christian salvation.

As he joyfully recalled his experiences with these Christians at Thessalonica, verse 3 states the reasons for his joyful recollection. Three famous words are in this verse, the trilogy of Christian virtues, "faith, hope, love" (cf. 1 Cor. 13:13). Since 1 Thessalonians was either Paul's earliest letter or one of the earliest, this was the first time in his writings that these words appeared together. Paul was not thanking the Lord simply because in the Thessalonians there was faith, hope, and love, which certainly ought to characterize every Christian. He was thanking God for what these three things had produced.

Of course no one can see faith, love, or hope; they are immaterial qualities. But they can be manifested and expressed in definite, tangible ways. They show themselves in life, and that is what is referred to here. The first two concepts, faith and works, are often contrasted—especially in Paul's later epistles. But here they are joined together; that is, a true faith is manifested in what we do. A true faith produces works. That is why James wrote that faith without works is dead (James 2:26). Not that works are a substitute for faith, but true faith in Christ brings a salvation that will in turn change the life and works of the believer.

Not only was a work of faith evident among the Thessalonians, but also a labor of love.

Love is more than a sentiment. It is a driving, motivating force in the heart of the believer who loves the Lord, and because he loves the Lord he is willing to labor; he is willing to work where it is difficult; and he is willing to bear the burden.

Added to the labor of love is "steadfastness of hope," that is, hope that produces patience. What kind of hope is it that produces patience? This is a calm, sure, trusting hope. Christians can have patience in hope because they are sure their hope in Christ will be fulfilled. Thus it was in the Thessalonian church. They not only hoped in God, but their hope produced patience in their hearts even in the time of trial and affliction which had overtaken them. Charles Swindoll summarizes the visible fruit that was produced in the lives of the Thessalonians. "The Thessalonians' unseen attitudes of faith, love, and hope were like hidden roots that produced the fruit of good works, loving labor, and patient endurance. How lush and fragrant these qualities were in Paul's memory now that he was so many miles away. . . . In his heart he carried with him a bouquet of encouragement, gathered from his brief encounter with the Thessalonian believers."[1]

The mention of faith, love, and hope and what they produce is so significant that some have used verse 3 as an outline for the rest of the book.

OUTLINE BASED ON 1 THESSALONIANS 1:3

I. The Work of Faith (1:1–3:13)   **Past**
II. The Labor of Love (4:1–12)   **Present**
III. The Steadfastness of Hope (4:13–5:28)   **Prospect**

Verse 3 concludes with something that is most significant. It tells us that Paul regarded the Thessalonians' work of faith, labor of love, and steadfastness of hope in Christ not simply as the way he saw these things, but as they were in the sight of God. This brings us to a pointed question that all of us can ask ourselves: What does God see in our hearts? A real trust in Him? A real love for Him? A real hope for that which is a part of our Christian faith? Paul saw the outward evidence of these things in the lives of the believers at Thessalonica, but God looks at the heart. Paul was able to commend these Christians as he remembered not only what he saw, but what he knew God saw. God looked not just to them, but through them into their hearts and lives.

PAUL'S KNOWLEDGE OF THE THESSALONIANS (1:4–6)

1:4–6 For we know, brothers loved by God, that he has chosen you, because our gospel came to you not only in word, but also in power and in the Holy Spirit and with full conviction. You know what kind of men we proved to be among you for your sake. And you became imitators of us and of the Lord, for you received the word in much affliction, with the joy of the Holy Spirit.

The second great theme of Paul's thankfulness to God was what he *knew* about these believers. He knew these things about them because they had trusted in God and received His wonderful salvation. In verse 4 Paul called attention to this with a reference to their election by God. How can a person know that someone else is chosen by God, that he or she is one of the elect of God? Considering the fact that Paul and Silas had ministered to these Christians only a few weeks or months, it is amazing that these believers were taught the doctrine of election.

Many modern-day Christians who have gone to church all their lives know very little about election and many other major Bible doctrines. The Bible indicates that God not only saves us, but that He chose us before the foundation of the world (Eph. 1:4). Election is a doctrine often not understood completely but believed because the Bible teaches it. Christians are the elect of God because God chose them before they chose Him (John 15:16; Rom. 9:10–23). While much mystery exists in divine sovereignty and human responsibility that we will never fully understand here on earth, the doctrine of election can be boiled down to one simple question—who makes the first move, God or man? Scripture teaches that God makes the first move (John 6:44). He draws the sinner to Himself and imparts salvation by His matchless grace.

But this raises another question: How can anyone know the elect of God? Who of us has ever seen the Book of Life? How can anyone really know that another person is one of God's elect? Verses 4–6 give the basis of Paul's confidence in connection with the Thessalonians and, at the same time, the basis for our faith and assurance that God is able to save those who trust in Christ. For example, one reason Paul believed the Thessalonians were saved, and why he knew their election was of God, was the way the gospel had come to them (v. 5). It came "in power and in the Holy Spirit and with full conviction" or assurance—literally, "in full measure." Their salvation had not been simply an emotional experience, nor had they been swept off their feet by Paul's scintillating oratory. This was unmistakably the Spirit's power at work in the hearts of both Paul and his new converts. Further, it had been confirmed by the way Paul and his companions had lived among them (v. 6). God's power had been clearly manifested in their lives as well as in their testimony.

The crowning evidence was in the way the Word was received. Preaching the Word is one thing; receiving it is another. In verse 6 three things are highlighted concerning the way they received the Word. First, they received it in such a way that they became followers of Paul and "imitators of us and of the Lord." Second, they received the Word in deep affliction. They did not receive the Word because it was easy to receive; they received it in spite of the persecution they knew would follow. Third, they received the Word with the joy of the Holy Spirit. In other words, in spite of affliction and trial there was the evidence of the Spirit's ministry in their hearts because they had the unspeakable joy that comes from the Holy Spirit. The Word was received in such a way that they knew and Paul knew they were really saved.

THE THESSALONIANS' GOOD TESTIMONY (1:7–10)

1:7–8 So that you became an example to all the believers in Macedonia and in Achaia. For not only has the word of the Lord sounded forth from you in Macedonia and Achaia, but your faith in God has gone forth everywhere, so that we need not say anything.

Verses 7–8 are the capstone of it all. Not only had the Thessalonians received the Word of God, but their salvation was manifested in their lives and testimony: Because they had really trusted in Christ, their salvation resulted in such a transformation of their lives that they became examples to all who believe.

The word "example" is the Greek word *tupos* from which we get our word "type." This term originally referred to the mark left by a blow and came to mean "image" or "pattern." These new believers served as a pattern or example; they were being used by God to "shape the lives of all the other believers in Greece."[2] Thessalonica was the chief city of Macedonia, which is northern Greece. And Achaia, the southern part of Greece, had Corinth as its principal city. Paul was writing to the Thessalonians from Corinth. This model church, however, was not just a pattern for all the other Greek churches. Paul added that the group was so alive and active that everyone knew what was going on in their church.

In other words, Paul was not required to tell people about how wonderfully God had been working in the Thessalonian church. The testimony went out everywhere without his help. People all over Greece had heard of their testimony and were following their example. One reason for this was that Thessalonica was on a major trade route, the Egnatian Way, and people passing through Thessalonica came in contact with the aggressive evangelism and testimony of these Christians who lived there.

In our day many people come and go in our cities and towns and never come in contact with any vital Christianity. That apparently was not true in Thessalonica, for as the Word spread it was widely known that God had done a wonderful work. The Thessalonians were preaching the Word, and the testimony of their faith in the Lord was reverberating throughout all of Greece. As Swindoll says, "As Paul moved through Macedonia, where Thessalonica was located, and Achaia, where Corinth was located, he would start to proclaim the gospel, then stop short in amazement. Still echoing down the canyons and through the streets was the word of the Lord spoken by the Thessalonian believers. Their Christianity was contagious and spreading faster than Paul could travel."[3]

> **1:9–10** For they themselves report concerning us the kind of reception we had among you, and how you turned to God from idols to serve the living and true God, and to wait for his Son from heaven, whom he raised from the dead, Jesus who delivers us from the wrath to come.

Timothy told Paul how God had worked in the Thessalonians after Paul and Silas had departed. They had turned to God from idols to serve the living and true God. This expression does not say they turned from idols to God. Rather, they turned *to* God *from* idols. They did not reform their ways first and then turn in faith to Christ. Instead they first placed their faith in Christ and then left their idols. Ray Stedman emphasizes the importance of this order. "You do not leave your idols for some reason and painfully try to find God. What happens is that you discover something of the beauty, the glory, and the greatness of God; and, seeing that and wanting it, you are willing to forsake the cheap and tawdry things you once believed could satisfy."[4]

The word "turned" in the Greek New Testament is in the aorist tense, which means that they turned once for all. It was a single, definite act. In a single, deliberate, decisive choice, they turned to God from idols. As a result of trusting in the living and true God, they served Him. Also of interest is the fact that the Thessalonians did not simply add Christ to their religious views. They did not make Him a part of their overall belief system. There was first addition and then subtraction. They added Christ and subtracted their idols.

Paul referred to the God they turned to, in contrast to their dead idols, as "the living and true God." Thessalonica is about fifty miles north of Mount

Olympus, the home of the pantheon of gods according to Greek mythology. Mount Olympus with its cloud-encircled peak is visible from Thessalonica on a clear day. The Thessalonians were steeped in pagan idolatry, yet the power of the gospel penetrated their lives as evidenced by their turning to the true God and turning their backs on idols. This indicates that the majority of the Thessalonian believers were Gentiles saved out of pagan religion.

As Paul thought about the faith and testimony of these Christians, young as they were, ignorant of many truths we know today, there was nevertheless assurance in his heart that they were really saved. He knew they were brothers and sisters in Christ, beloved of God; he knew they were elect of God by the evidence of the transforming work of salvation manifested in their changed lives.

These believers had salvation as was wonderfully manifested in their lives, but they also had a glorious hope. One of the most precious things about the Christian hope is that it goes on and on and on. Salvation is not limited to the present; it is also for the future. In verse 10 the truth of the Lord's coming is introduced—a truth prominent in every chapter in 1 Thessalonians.

Of significance is the fact that in such a brief period of ministry Paul not only led them out of darkness into the light in the gospel, but he also faithfully preached to them the truth of the Lord's coming. By contrast today, many people who go to church year after year never hear the precious truth that Christ who came to Bethlehem so long ago is coming again and that we can be looking for that wonderful return of the Lord for His own. How sad and unfortunate that preaching and teaching about the Lord's coming is seldom heard in many churches.

But Paul was faithful to present this hope to the early Christians. So in verse 10 he reminded the believers in Thessalonica that they not only had turned to God from idols (v. 9)—a present work—but they also had a new hope for the future: "To wait for his Son from heaven." The word "wait" is in the present tense. This expresses the notion of imminence; that is, Christ could come at any time. Many things *may* happen before He comes, but nothing must transpire before He can come. The Thessalonians had turned to God in one decisive act, but there remained the constant, day-by-day expectation of His return.

In other words, they were constantly looking for the return of the Lord at any time for His saints. The word "wait" is a compound word. It has a prefix attached to the beginning of the word that means "up." So we might translate verse 10, "and to *wait up* for his Son from heaven."[5] Like a parent anxiously waiting up for a teenage child to return home, or a wife waiting up for her husband to get home from a long trip, these believers were waiting up for their Lord's coming. Are we doing the same today?

The chapter closes with the reminder that the risen Lord Jesus Christ is the One who is coming (v. 10). In one short verse several great doctrines are gathered together: (1) Christ's second coming: to "wait for his Son from heaven"; (2) the resurrection of Christ: "whom he raised from the dead"; and (3) the salvation Christ purchased in His first coming when He died on the cross: "who delivers us from the wrath to come."

Wrath is coming! The closing chapter of 1 Thessalonians presents this fact very graphically. Some believe that "the wrath to come" here refers to God's eternal wrath in hell. This is possible in light of the preceding context that deals with their salvation. However, these believers would have already been well aware of their deliverance from that judgment. It seems better in light of what Paul would teach in 1 Thessalonians 5:1–9 about the coming time of wrath on earth and the mention of Christ's coming in 1:10 to take this as a reference to the future day of the Lord, the time of great tribulation.

Make no mistake. A day of judgment is coming, a time when God will judge this sinful world. Nearly two thousand years ago, Christ on Calvary delivered us from the wrath to come—that is, He delivered all who would trust in Him, all who would receive Him as their personal Savior. These Thessalonians who lived so long ago had come into the glorious truth that Christ had died for them. They were delivered from the coming wrath that will be part of the day of the Lord. This supports the pretribulation view for the timing of the Lord's coming that we will discuss in more detail in 1 Thessalonians 4–5. For these believers and for us the coming of the Lord is a glorious event we can look for each day with keen anticipation and with hearts filled with expectation.

First Thessalonians 1 constitutes a challenge to every thinking Christian. We are challenged to ask, What do people think of us when they pray for us? Do they remember our work of faith, our labor of love, and our steadfastness of hope? When they think of us, are they assured of our salvation? Do they see in our lives the evidence that the Word of God has come in power, that we have been transformed, that we have been made true followers of the Lord Jesus Christ, that we exercise our faith in the midst of affliction and trials, that we have the evidence of the joy of the Holy Spirit and a transformed life so that our testimony is spread abroad? Is that true of us?

And like the Thessalonians do we have the living hope of the Lord's coming, the same One who loved us, who died for our sins that He might deliver us from the wrath to come, and who was raised in victory over the grave? This letter was written many years ago to Christians who long since have left the earthly scene, but the truth lives on. May the truths of this chapter not only live in the written pages of God's Word, but may they also be manifested in our hearts and our daily lives.

NOTES

1. Charles R. Swindoll, *Contagious Christianity: A Study of I Thessalonians*, Bible Study Guide (Anaheim, CA: Insight for Living, 1993), 5.

2. Richard Mayhue, *First and Second Thessalonians: Triumphs and Trials of a Consecrated Church* (Fearn, Ross-shire, Scotland: Christian Focus, 1999), 55.

3. Swindoll, *Contagious Christianity,* 7.

4. Ray C. Stedman, *Waiting for the Second Coming: Studies in Thessalonians* (Grand Rapids: Discovery House, 1990), 15.

5. Charles Caldwell Ryrie, *First and Second Thessalonians,* Everyman's Bible Commentary (Chicago: Moody, 1959), 30.

2

Serving the Coming Lord
1 Thessalonians 2:1–20

The word *salvation* was written in big letters over the first chapter like a large banner because this letter would never have been written if the Thessalonians had not trusted in the Lord Jesus. Their salvation marked the beginning of vital living for God, of entering into eternal, spiritual things. This is a reminder, of course, that one does not begin living until he is saved by trusting the Lord Jesus Christ. Life begins when that greatest of all decisions is made of trusting in Jesus Christ as one's personal Savior.

Many today have religion; that is, they go to church and engage in religious activities. But many of them have only the outer appearance of Christianity and have never come to real faith in Jesus Christ as their Savior. The Thessalonians, however, were not guilty of superficial religion. They had truly trusted Christ, and their lives had been transformed. The fact of their salvation lays the firm foundation for the truths revealed in the chapters that follow.

Over chapter 2 can be written the very common word: service. The chapter reveals how to serve God both by precept and by Paul's dynamic example. First Thessalonians 2 is a glowing "success story." Paul had done something that was quite phenomenal. He had come to a thriving, major, pagan city where there was not a single Christian. He had gone into the Jewish synagogue and there had preached the gospel. He had preached also to Gentiles in their homes. In a few weeks this dynamic apostle by the grace of God had founded a new church—a church that has been known through the centuries to us as an example of faith and faithfulness. How did he do it?

BOLDNESS IN SPITE OF SUFFERING (2:1–2)

2:1–2 For you yourselves know, brothers, that our coming to you was not in vain. But though we had already suffered and been shamefully treated at Philippi, as you know, we had boldness in our God to declare to you the gospel of God in the midst of much conflict.

Many communities in America today desperately need churches that bear a real testimony for Christ. There is no shortage today of methodology, seminars, books, consultants, conferences, and demographic experts telling pastors and leaders how to do ministry and build big churches. But what does the Bible say about building a successful church? Can we have such churches? How can we have such churches? What are the building blocks of a ministry that lasts? The answers are found in the second chapter of 1 Thessalonians. Paul began this chapter with the fact that God had used him and Silas to found a thriving church in Thessalonica. "For you yourselves know, brothers, that our coming to you was not in vain." The word "vain" means hollow, empty, or a failure. This ministry was not a failure but a glowing success. God had undertaken for them and blessed the message and many were saved. In verse 2 the secret of this kind of ministry is revealed.

Over the first two verses of the second chapter we can write the word *boldness* or *courage*. One of the reasons Paul was successful was that he was bold. If he had gone to Thessalonica and had failed to preach the gospel, the probability is that in a few weeks he would not have made much of an impression. If he had not told anyone about the Lord Jesus Christ, if he had not proclaimed boldly that Jesus is the only Savior, that Christ loves the world, that He died for the world, that they could be saved only by trusting in the risen Savior, then he would not have had one convert.

The first point in effective service for God is boldness, a boldness made more significant by subjection to suffering. Paul and Silas had come from Philippi where they had been beaten and thrown into prison (Acts 16:22–24), suffering intensely for the gospel's sake. But when Paul came to Thessalonica, instead of saying "I have suffered enough," "I will go back home and wait for a better time to preach," or "I will tone down my message and make it less offensive and more palatable"—as some Christians might have done— he pressed on and spoke boldly and courageously.

The word translated "bold" in verse 2 comes from a Greek word of eight syllables, *eparrēsiasametha*. This long word means to be bold in the sense of speaking out. Undoubtedly some people who are saved have not told very many others about it. But secret believers do not lead others to Christ. The way to lead people to Christ is to be *bold*, to proclaim the gospel unashamedly. This is the basic program of the present age or dispensation.

Paul was called to preach and he did so boldly, "in the midst of much conflict." The word translated "conflict" is *agoni*, from which comes the word *agony*. The Greek word *agoni* was used of the intense struggle an athlete puts forth to win first place in a race or a contest.[1] There was an agony or strong opposition around Paul as he preached, but there was also an agony of soul in Paul as he preached the gospel. To be effective in our testimony, to be successful even by worldly standards, it is necessary to have a boldness inspired by an agony of heart. This does not mean that one should be tactless, or without common sense in one's approach, but there must be a bold witness for Jesus Christ.

PREACHING THE PURE WORD (2:3–6)

2:3–6 For our appeal does not spring from error or impurity or any attempt to deceive, but just as we have been approved by God to be entrusted with the gospel, so we speak, not to please man, but to please God who tests our hearts. For we never came with words of flattery, as you know, nor with a pretext for greed— God is witness. Nor did we seek glory from people, whether from you or from others, though we could have made demands as apostles of Christ.

These verses graphically portray the character of Paul's preaching. One tragedy of our day, as all true Bible students know, is that some preaching is not according to the Word of God. Modern Christians need to be like the ancient Bereans, who were the next people Paul and Silas visited after being forced out of Thessalonica (Acts 17:10–11). The Bereans "examin[ed] the Scriptures daily to see if these things were so" (v. 11). Believers today need to search the Scriptures, testing the messages they hear by the Book.

By this standard Paul's preaching to the Thessalonians rang true. This was evident first by the things that were not true about his preaching. In verses 3–6, he referred to the purity of his message in its *content* and its *intent*. It was pure in the sense that there was no deceit or literally, no error. There was no uncleanness or impurity of motive either. Paul did not preach the gospel to enrich himself.

Sometimes truth is mixed with error. In fact, the most dangerous kind of preaching is what is partly true. But Paul said, "My message was not just partly true. It is without error. It has no deceit in it. It is the pure truth. It is not adulterated by human philosophy and human speculation." It was God's pure message to them concerning Christ.

Paul went on to make a further claim: his message was also without guile or deceit—that is, he did not come to trick them and to use methods that were questionable. He did not try to get superficial decisions for Christ, but he laid down plainly before them the truth of the gospel and the issues of heaven and hell. The result was that when they trusted in Christ, it was a clear-cut decision that resulted in a strong testimony that stood the test in the days that followed. It depended on the purity of the message in both its content and intent.

Paul was a faithful servant of God as he preached. He made it clear that his motive in preaching was "not to please man, but to please God who tests our hearts" (v. 4). The final test of every life and of every message or sermon is, "What does God think about it?" The judgment of God is not always according to human judgment. People may judge a message by its interest, its humor, its literary quality, the words delivered, its intelligence, the fact that the speaker revealed great background of knowledge in his subject, or by the skill and precision with which it was delivered. Of course when a preacher delivers a message for God it should be as good as he can make it. God is not pleased by sloppy preparation and careless presentation of His Word. But God is primarily concerned with the message itself. Is it true? The most beautifully delivered sermon that is not true, or is only partly true, is not God's message and therefore is useless in the hands of God and poisonous to the hearers.

Again the ultimate test of a message is, Does it please God? That is true for the preacher, for the Sunday school teacher, for the Bible study teacher, and for the person engaged in one-on-one evangelism or discipleship. The most basic test of any service rendered for God is the question, "Is it pleasing to Him?" Our little houses of self-praise and self-gratification tumble in a moment when we stop to consider, "What does God think about it?" As Paul preached he said, "I was not trying to please you Thessalonians; I did not come here to impress upon you that I was a great pulpit orator, a great missionary, or a great scholar. I was here because I was seeking to please God." Paul was not a shallow, insecure people-pleaser. Of course, good leaders must strive to get along well with others, but this must not be the driving force. Paul was energized and propelled by a burning desire to please God. Certainly this is a standard to challenge every thoughtful Christian.

In verse 5 Paul revealed how this worked: "For we never came with words of flattery, as you know, nor with a pretext for greed—God is witness." As was mentioned earlier in chapter 1, sometimes Paul appealed to the outward— that is, what *people* can see—and other times he appealed to what *God* can see. It is not difficult for us to identify flattery. We all know people who are flatterers, and sometimes we like to listen to them. Some people delight to be told, "My, you look so young," and to hear that they look fifteen years younger than they actually are. The flesh loves flattery. It has been well said that gossip is saying something behind someone's back that you would never say to his face, while flattery is saying something to someone's face that you would never say behind his back.

Paul rejected all flattery. He said, "I did not come to you and say, what outstanding citizens you are! What beautiful characters you are! People as good as you are ought to be trusting Christ." No, he told them the hard truth: that they were lost sinners, that they were bound for hell, that they desperately needed a Savior, and that their religion was not enough. They needed Christ; they needed His glorious salvation. There was no flattery, no Christian salesmanship or manipulation in Paul's message. It was the unvarnished truth. He did not come to flatter the Thessalonians or appeal to their ego. He came to deliver a message from God, and he reminded them of the fact that they knew it. No one in Thessalonica thought of Paul as a flatterer.

People can hear a person's words; but when it comes to greed, this pertains to the heart. One cannot always tell whether a person is greedy or not. It is difficult to determine whether one is serving you to make money or whether he is honestly trying to help you without greedy motives. Paul did something here that is certainly the application of the acid test; he called on God to witness that he and Silas ministered from pure motives. Paul was saying, "God is my witness, Silas and I did not come here to make merchandise of you; we did not come because you promised us a generous honorarium, a high salary, or any of the other comforts of life. We did not come that way to you and you know it. God is witness that our hearts were right in this thing." Not only was Paul's message pure in its content, but his whole purpose was pure in the sight of God. That, of course, was one of the reasons God could use him.

Verse 6 adds another important factor: "Nor did we seek glory from people, whether from you or from others, though we could have made demands as apostles of Christ." Paul could have come to the Thessalonians, puffed out his chest, and said, "I am an apostle and you must recognize my high office because God has sent me." He could have demanded "first-class treatment" and thrown his weight around in an authoritarian fashion.[2] He could have told them he had the right to order them around.

But instead Paul said, "I did not come in that spirit. I did not come to be honored by you. I came because I had a message, because I wanted to help you, because you needed the Savior." Paul refused to be put on a pedestal. He came to humbly serve the people. Certainly that is the secret of an effective Christian testimony. Boldness, having our hearts right before God, delivering God's message in its purity and in its power, seeking not our own advantage but seeking the glory and approval of God—that is the secret of

Paul's success. And it will be the success of any person who wishes to truly serve the Lord.

SIX MINISTRY BUSTERS (1 THESS. 2:3–6)

Error

Ulterior, deceptive motives

Flattery

Greed

People-pleasing

Authoritarian attitude (glory for self)

LOVING THE PEOPLE OF GOD (2:7–12)

2:7–12 But we were gentle among you, like a nursing mother taking care of her own children. So, being affectionately desirous of you, we were ready to share with you not only the gospel of God but also our own selves, because you had become very dear to us. For you remember, brothers, our labor and toil: we worked night and day, that we might not be a burden to any of you, while we proclaimed to you the gospel of God. You are witnesses, and God also, how holy and righteous and blameless was our conduct toward you believers. For you know how, like a father with his children, we exhorted each one of you and encouraged you and charged you to walk in a manner worthy of God, who calls you into his own kingdom and glory.

In verses 1–6 Paul itemized the things that he *did not do.* He was not greedy or deceitful, and he did not have errors in his message. Now in verses

7–12 we have what he did do—the positive side of his message. There is a danger of regarding Christianity as a negative standard: Don't do this; don't do that; don't do something else. There are bona fide negatives in the Christian faith. If one is to have a genuine testimony for Christ, there are some things he cannot do. We have just seen several of them highlighted in verses 1–6. But Christianity consists not in negatives, but in what one believes, in the life one lives, and in the service one renders. Paul revealed here the secret of why he was so effective in Thessalonica.

In verses 7–8, Paul used the imagery of a nursing mother to describe his loving care for these believers. Here was the compassionate heart that made possible Paul's successful ministry. He was taking care of them just as a new mother takes care of her baby—even being willing, if necessary, to give her own life for her child, which Paul also was willing to do for the Thessalonians. This was not hyperbole; it revealed the burning heart Paul had as he dealt with these whom he had led to know Jesus Christ as Savior.

Paul's love for the Thessalonians raises a key question. Have we lost our heart in our service for God? Sometimes we do things for God because it is our duty. If we cannot do it for any other reason, let us do it as our duty. But certainly there is something deeper than that. Paul had come to the city of Thessalonica, to people he had never seen before. But how he loved them now as trophies of grace! As a parent loves his child, he loved these little ones of Christ.

Paul also reminded the Thessalonians that he had worked hard when he was with them (v. 9). Paul did not have a forty-hour work week. When it came to 4:30 or 5:00 in the afternoon, he did not say, "The rest of the day is mine; I can do with it as I please." No, Paul was a bond-slave of Jesus Christ. He was under orders like a soldier, whether his ministry required eight or twelve or twenty-four hours a day. Paul was on duty, and he realized that his time was short. So he "worked night and day."

In apostolic times it was customary to stop work when darkness came and to go to bed. A person who worked night and day was unusual, but that was what Paul did. Many a lonely hour in the night he was praying with them, trying to help some soul come to Christ, seeking to understand the tremendous issues that were latent in the gospel message. Also, many times Paul was alone on his knees before God, getting the power, strength, and wisdom to know what to do the next day as he sought to be a true servant of God. The Christian life is not a continuous vacation. Christians should have periodic vacations even as Christ took His disciples off to rest awhile. We all need times to relax, recharge, and revive. It is important to take time periodically to "sharpen the ax." But the Christian life should not be a question of doing as little as possible. Rather, like Paul our lives should be poured out in dedicated service for the Lord.

In verses 10–11, Paul changed the figure of a nursing mother caring for her child to that of a father who loves his children. Both of these images accurately portrayed the apostle's heart for the Thessalonians. The words "each of you" remind us that true ministry is personal. Just as a father knows his children and how to deal with them differently, so we too must deal with people as individuals.

Paul's ministry was honorable before God who sees the heart. Seeking to win others for Christ is not only a matter of boldness in the spoken message. There must also be the corresponding life of testimony for God. Few Christians realize how many are watching them to discover in their lives the answer to the question of whether Christianity is real, whether it really satisfies, and whether it pays to serve the Lord. Paul delivered the message in word and in life as he ministered to the Thessalonians. His daily life before them was that of a man who was walking in the will of God.

Paul concluded this section, therefore, in verse 12: "We exhorted each one of you and encouraged you and charged you to walk in a manner worthy of God, who calls you into his own kingdom and glory." Christians are in the kingdom of God now, but there is a glorious kingdom ahead of us also, the glory that will be ours in the predicted millennial kingdom and throughout eternity as we are with Christ (Revelation 20–22). In view of these things, God has called us to a walk that is in keeping with our destiny. A child born into a royal family is given special care. He cannot do the things that other children do, at least not in quite the same way. The reason is that he is being prepared for a place of responsibility and leadership.

Christians are in exactly that same position. We do not "walk worthy" in order to be saved, or in order to become a royal child, but we are to "walk worthy" of God because we are saved, because we are children of the King by grace through faith in the Lord Jesus Christ. So Paul laid before the Thessalonian Christians this exhortation to "walk worthy." This standard can solve many problems! Sometimes people will come to a preacher or a Sunday school teacher and say: "Now, is this right? Can a Christian do this?" So many of those problems are solved in a moment if we ask the simple question: "Is it worthy? Is it something that is honoring to God? Would God be pleased with this situation?" Often the uncertainties and obscurities in human judgment are wiped away when one applies the test of the Scriptures. Certainly there are many things that we cannot do as Christians because we are Christians, because God has called us to a holy walk and a life that is well pleasing to Him.

RECEIVING THE WORD AS FROM GOD (2:13–16)

2:13–16 And we also thank God constantly for this, that when you received the word of God, which you heard from us, you accepted it not as the word of men but as what it really is, the word of God, which is at work in you believers. For you, brothers, became imitators of the churches of God in Christ Jesus that are in Judea. For you suffered the same things from your own countrymen as they did from the Jews, who killed both the Lord Jesus and the prophets, and drove us out, and displease God and oppose all mankind by hindering us from speaking to the Gentiles that they might be saved—so as always to fill up the measure of their sins. But God's wrath has come upon them at last!

In the closing portion of chapter 2, the other side of the picture is presented. In the first twelve verses Paul's secret of success was unfolded—why he preached, how he preached, and why he had such phenomenal results. Two aspects to every sermon are the delivery and the hearing. The preacher or teacher has a responsibility to accurately deliver the message in a way that is relevant and interesting, but the congregation has an equal responsibility to joyfully listen, receive, and apply the truth.

We listen to sermons from different standpoints. A preacher may listen to a sermon to see if he can get a message or a helpful illustration for some future occasion. A Sunday school teacher may listen to a sermon to see if he can get some information for his lesson. A person who is lonely may be coming for comfort. The unsaved may be seeking salvation. There are different motives behind our hearing, not all of which are good. Sometimes Christians do not come with open hearts to receive a message from God. They become occupied with the messenger instead of the message and the Savior. As Jesus taught in the parable of the sower, the degree to which the seed of God's Word takes root and produces fruit in the life of a person is directly related to the degree of preparation in the soil of the heart (Matt. 13:1–9, 18–23). Only prepared hearts receive and respond to the message of truth. The believers at Thessalonica had hearts of "good soil" that were primed to hear God's Word and produced a rich harvest.

But the Thessalonians were not simply interested in Paul, as grand a figure as he was. They also received the message he delivered as the Word of God (v. 13). The message was received not because Paul delivered it. The thing that thrilled them was that they had heard God's Word. They had received it as the authoritative Word of God because it came from God. The proof of this is found in the verses that follow.

One of the surprising effects of God's Word is its power "to arouse violent opposition."[3] This has been true from the very first generation of believers. Testing had come almost at once for this new band of Christians, and they were bitterly persecuted. Paul told them in verses 14–15 that they became followers of others who were persecuted before them. One of the most difficult experiences in life is when you stand for Christ and your own loved ones oppose you. If friends, neighbors, and relatives—one's own loved ones—oppose a young Christian, this is extremely difficult, but this was often true in the early church. This is also true in modern times in many parts of the world. What a young Christian does under these circumstances is a test of the reality of his faith. The Thessalonians had stood true, no matter who opposed them.

Persecution was not peculiar to the Thessalonians, however. Paul related that those who lived in Jerusalem at that time had "killed both the Lord Jesus and the prophets, and drove us out, and displease God and oppose all mankind." Paul, who was a Jew, was being persecuted by his fellow country-men just as Christ had been crucified by His own people. The Thessalonians were going through a similar experience. Opposition to the apostles had gone so far as to be described in verse 16 as "hindering us from speaking to the Gentiles that they might be saved—so as always to fill up the measure of their sins. But God's wrath has come upon them at last."

Some have accused the apostle Paul here of engaging in anti-Semitism, but this is a false charge. Paul knew better than anyone the bitter hatred some Jews had for Christians. He had been on both sides of the fence (cf. Acts 8:1). He had been the hunter and the hunted. What he said here about the Jewish people of his day was simply a factual indictment of their actions. Jesus also pronounced judgment on the Jews for their unbelief (Matt. 23:35), and He was certainly not anti-Semitic. The persecution Paul faced in Thessalonica was instigated by the Jews (Acts 17:5). However, we must never forget Paul's deep love and longing for the salvation of his people, the Jews (Rom. 9:1–5; 10:1; 11:1).

There are several views on Paul's statement about the Jews that "God's wrath has come upon them at last." Some take this to refer to the destruction of the temple in Jerusalem in A.D. 70 that was looming on the near horizon. But this wouldn't directly affect Jews in Thessalonica, who had persecuted Paul (cf. Acts 17:5–9). Others take it to refer to the wrath of the future tribu-lation or the eternal wrath of hell since there is so much in the Thessalonian letters about the coming wrath. However, the text says that this wrath has already come upon them. In the Greek the verb "has come upon" is in the aorist (past) tense. Those who take this as the future tribulation or eternal wrath of hell note that this is stated in the past tense because it is so certain to occur it can be stated as if it has already begun. While this view is possible, the best view is that this refers to God's wrath in the form of spiritual blindness and hardness of heart that had come upon the majority of the Jews because of their unbelief (Rom. 11:7–10, 25).

The key point here, however, is that the opposition of the world and of the unbelieving heart is especially brought out when a person faithfully preaches Christ. The world, Jew and Gentile, does not necessarily oppose morality as such. Nor does it oppose religion as such, but it does oppose a bona fide, transforming kind of Christianity. The world does not want Christ and Him crucified. It does not want a gospel that ignores human merit, exposes human pride, and calls sinners to trust in Christ and Him alone for salvation and forgiveness. When we take our stand for Christ and His Word, we can expect some opposition from unbelievers.

PAUL'S LONGING FOR THE THESSALONIANS (2:17–18)

2:17–18 But since we were torn away from you, brothers, for a short time, in person not in heart, we endeavored the more eagerly and with great desire to see you face to face, because we wanted to come to you—I, Paul, again and again—but Satan hindered us.

Paul opened his heart again as he told the Thessalonian believers how much he longed to see them. Paul had been quickly torn away from those new believers at Thessalonica as a result of the persecution that was stirred up by the Jews. The words "torn away" literally mean "orphaned." Paul and Silas had been expelled from Thessalonica suddenly and separated from their dear children in the faith. Paul longed to see them again.

When we have loved ones who are away from us and we get word that they are going through the deep waters of affliction, how we want to drop everything and rush to them! We think they need us, and our comfort and help. Paul was just that way, but he could not go back. Some maintain that his inability to return to Thessalonica was because of some physical illness (2 Cor. 12:7; Gal. 4:15). Although this is possible, it seems foreign to the context. In light of the background information we have about Thessalonica in Acts 17, it seems better to hold that Paul's return would have cost Jason and others the bond they had secured and would have added to their affliction (Acts 17:9). Moreover, if Paul had gone back, he probably would have become a martyr for the faith. He would have cut short a ministry that God had for him. It was not God's will for Paul to die at this point in his life. For this reason he could not go to Thessalonica.

Satan, which means "adversary," hindered Paul. How Satan sometimes gets in our way! This word "hinder" in the Greek was used in a military sense of breaking up a road to block the way for an opposing army. The thought is that the way back to Thessalonica for Paul was impassable. Satan had broken up the road before him, and Paul could not get through to them, even though he longed to see them and be a further help to them. Paul knew firsthand the intensity and ferocity of spiritual warfare.

Satan is constantly at work in churches trying to wreak destruction, divisions, and discouragement. As Richard Mayhue notes, "Someone has said, 'When God is at work, Satan is surely alongside.' What Christ was building (Matt. 16:18), the devil was committed to destroying. It is not surprising then to see Satan so visible in so many New Testament churches, e.g. Jerusalem (Acts 5:1–10), Corinth (2 Cor. 2:1–11), Ephesus (1 Tim. 3:6–7), Smyrna (Rev. 2:9–10), Pergamum (Rev. 2:13), Thyatira (Rev. 2:24), and Philadelphia (Rev. 3:9)."[4] The Thessalonian church can be added to this list, but it is comforting to recognize that God used even the opposition of Satan to accomplish His own good purposes. Had Paul been able to travel back to Thessalonica, we would not have the two letters to the Thessalonians in our Bible. Our sovereign God always overcomes the works of the enemy.

PAUL'S HOPE AND JOY (2:19–20)

2:19–20 For what is our hope or joy or crown of boasting before our Lord Jesus at his coming? Is it not you? For you are our glory and joy.

After the sobering description of Satan's hindrance, Paul wanted the Thessalonians to know that all was not lost. There is a bright note, repeated so often in this epistle—the triumphant theme of the coming of the Lord and the joy that will be ours when Christ comes back. We can ask with Paul in verse 19, "What is our hope?" What does the future hold for us? Do we have a real hope? Yes, one who has been born again, who is a child of God, has a real hope. But if our hope is not in Christ we have no basis for hope.

Paul also asked, "What is our joy or crown of boasting?" He looked forward to the glad day when this life's journey would be over and he would be in the presence of the Lord along with all the other Christians. Paul was picturing the rapture of the church, when Christ will come for His own to take them home to glory and all believers will appear before the judgment seat of Christ to receive reward or loss of reward (2 Cor. 5:10).

The answer to this question for Paul was believers like the Thessalonians. The apostle was not content to be saved himself. It is wonderful to be saved; it is wonderful to know one is going to heaven. But Paul said the real joy that would be in his heart as he stood in the presence of the Lamb of God, the One who loved him, the One who had died for him on the cross, would be his spiritual children whom he would bring with him, whom he had led to know Jesus Christ as their Savior.

Have you ever led another person to Christ? You might say, "I'm not an evangelist. I'm not good at sharing my faith with others." But have you ever tried? Not all believers are evangelists, not all have the spiritual gift of evangelism, but every believer is called to be a witness for Christ. God loves to use those who are willing to be used, and there is latent in many Christians a gift for leading people to Christ which they may not realize.

Almost anyone can give out gospel tracts. Any Christian can pray. Anyone can give of his substance for missions. Anyone can invite a person to a church service where the gospel will be clearly presented. God can use us in many ways to lead others to Christ if we are serious about it. When that glad day comes when we are in the presence of Christ at the judgment seat, will we have some trophies of grace? Paul said, "When that day comes, I am going to be exalted. I am going to be rewarded. Why? Because of you Thessalonians who came to know the Lord Jesus Christ through my ministry among you."

In that day will we be able to look at those saved through our gospel testimony and say with Paul, "You are our glory and joy"?

NOTES

1. Robert L. Thomas, "1 Thessalonians," in *The Expositor's Bible Commentary*, gen. ed. Frank E. Gaebelein, vol. 11 (Grand Rapids: Zondervan, 1978), 250.

2. Charles R. Swindoll, *Contagious Christianity: A Study of I Thessalonians*, Bible Study Guide (Anaheim, CA: Insight for Living, 1993), 15.

3. Ray C. Stedman, *Waiting for the Second Coming: Studies in Thessalonians* (Grand Rapids: Discovery House, 1990), 42.

4. Richard Mayhue, *First and Second Thessalonians: Triumphs and Trials of a Consecrated Church* (Fearn, Ross-shire, Scotland: Christian Focus, 1999), 88.

Blameless in Holiness
1 Thessalonians 3:1–4:12

In the first chapter of 1 Thessalonians, the great theme of *salvation* was unfolded. There is nothing in all the world that thrills the heart like a real experience of trust in the Lord Jesus, which the Thessalonians had experienced. Chapter 2 presented the challenge of Christian service. Paul spoke of his own *service* and the solid building blocks of successful ministry, as well as the service and faithfulness of the Thessalonian church as it will be recognized at the judgment seat of Christ in glory. Chapter 3 presents the theme of *sanctification*, which continues through 4:12.

GOOD NEWS FROM THESSALONICA (3:1–7)

3:1–7 Therefore when we could bear it no longer, we were willing to be left behind at Athens alone, and we sent Timothy, our brother and God's coworker in the gospel of Christ, to establish and exhort you in your faith, that no one be moved by these afflictions. For you yourselves know that we are destined for this. For when we were with you, we kept telling you beforehand that we were to suffer affliction, just as it has come to pass, and just as you know. For this reason, when I could bear it no longer, I sent to learn about your faith, for fear that somehow the tempter had tempted you and our labor would be in vain. But now that Timothy has come to us from you, and has brought us the good news of your faith and love and reported that you always remember us kindly and long to see us, as we long to see you—for this reason, brothers, in all our distress and affliction we have been comforted about you through your faith.

In 1 Thessalonians 3:1–7, Paul related the testimony of the Thessalonian church as it was brought to him. In a word, this is what happened. When Paul was meditating on the need of the Thessalonian church and his heart was burdened in prayer for them, he had sent Timothy, "our brother and God's coworker in the gospel of Christ," back to find out how they were getting along. The purpose of Timothy's visit was "to establish, and exhort you in your faith, that no one be moved by these afflictions." Timothy was to do what Paul longed to do himself, but could not. Paul wanted the Thessalonians to continue steadfast in spite of affliction, which Paul reminded them they were "destined" to suffer. He was concerned lest the trial uncover superficiality in their faith and "for fear that somehow the tempter had tempted you and our labor would be in vain." This is the second mention of Satan ("the tempter") in Thessalonians. His evil work will be presented again in 2 Thessalonians 2:9 in conjunction with the coming Antichrist.

SATAN IN THE THESSALONIAN EPISTLES

Satan the hinderer (1 Thessalonians 2:18)

Satan the tempter (1 Thessalonians 3:5)

Satan the deceiver (2 Thessalonians 2:9)

Timothy had gone to Thessalonica and had brought encouragement to them, continuing to teach the Word of God. Now Timothy had returned to Paul with the message that these believers were standing fast in the faith, that they longed to see Paul, and that they were just as he had left them—their hearts fixed on the Lord Jesus Christ and looking for His coming. Paul's heart overflowed with joy and thanksgiving as he contemplated the goodness of God in blessing his testimony there and working so abundantly in the lives of these Thessalonians (3:6–7).

PAUL'S GREAT HEART (3:8-10)

3:8-10 For now we live, if you are standing fast in the Lord. For what thanksgiving can we return to God for you, for all the joy that we feel for your sake before our God, as we pray most earnestly night and day that we may see you face to face and supply what is lacking in your faith?

A number of things could be said about this portion of Scripture. Paul recited how he was comforted, his whole spiritual joy and happiness being linked with the experience of victory in this Thessalonian church. Consider for a moment the background of verse 8. How interested and how concerned would we be if we had been in Paul's position? He had been there just a few weeks (Acts 17:1–3) and had led these few souls to Christ, but now it seems that his very life depended on the success of this church. His whole heart was wrapped up in the spiritual prosperity of these his children in the faith. Paul carried the concern for the churches he founded in his heart wherever he traveled (2 Cor. 11:28–29). Swindoll says it well, "You will recall that a wave of persecution had forced the Apostle away from the Christians in Thessalonica. As he traveled to other cities, he worried about these new believers like a parent who tosses and turns in the night, concerned about his faraway children."[1]

What a challenge this should be to us that we may have that same sensitivity of heart, that same passion, that same love that was in the heart of Christ Himself for His sheep, the people of God. In the Bible, men who really served God had a heart for the needs of souls. Too often in our modern life our theology is in one compartment and our heart is in another. We believe that souls are lost without Christ and we recognize human suffering and human need, but it is too seldom translated into prayer, or into helpfulness, or into doing what we can to meet the needs of others. What a contrast to Paul!

Verses 9 and 10 present another graphic picture of Paul's great heart. The words "pray most earnestly" (*deomenoi*) mean literally "to beg or ask a favor." They express an attitude of total dependence on God. Here is the

compassionate heart of Paul toward the Thessalonian believers and his concern lest they lack something in their spiritual faith and experience. Modern
Christians are so prone to ignore a need like this. While recognizing that
so many Christians are ignorant of the great truths of Scripture and are not
going on with the Lord, they do not have a real prayer life; they do not
give themselves to the study of the Word; they are not soul winners. How
tragic that in our hearts there can be such coldness and such a lack of
response to spiritual need.

What a challenge Paul gives us! In his spiritual experience his heart was
overflowing in praise to God for hearing his prayer. It was not just a few min-
utes or a few sentences of prayer; he spent hours, day and night, praying to
God for the continuance and faithfulness of this little band of Christians. If
we prayed like that, and if our hearts were stirred like Paul's, we would have
a spiritual revival such as this nation has never seen. What we need is revival
first in the hearts of the people of God.

What does Paul say to us in this passage? He is saying that if we are really
committed to the Lord—if we are letting the Holy Spirit rule supremely in
our hearts and lives—there should be the evidence of the love and compas-
sion of the Holy Spirit toward our fellow Christians as well as toward those
who do not know the Lord Jesus. The challenge of this passage is to let the
Spirit transform our hearts and make them tender, that we may not follow the
pattern of this careless and indifferent generation which is unmindful of the
spiritual needs of those about us.

Are we genuinely concerned about others? Do we pray for the salvation
of that neighbor in the next apartment or in the next house? Are we concerned in our churches about the backsliders and those who are indifferent
toward serving the Lord as they should? We learn from Paul that the secret
is to pray. If we have a real burden of prayer, we will have Paul's experience of
the joy of answered prayer. Certainly these are important and most practical
verses.

Before we leave this section, we need to note this important phrase in
verse 10: "That we may . . . supply what is lacking in your faith." The King
James Version rendered the verb "supply" as "perfect." Even though this word

has been more accurately rendered as "supply" or "complete" in newer English translations, the presence of the word "perfect" has helped lead to confusion on the part of those who think that it is not possible to be saved unless one reaches a stage of moral perfection. They attribute to the word "perfect" ideas that are contrary to the Word of God. What did Paul mean here? It seems clear that he was not doubting their salvation because he said, "For we know, brothers loved by God, that he has chosen you" (1:4).

There are two main ideas about perfection in the Bible: (1) first is the idea of coming to the end of a journey or the fulfillment of a purpose or a design. It is fulfillment or perfection in the sense, for instance, of a perfect man, one who has grown through boyhood and youth until he has the full stature of a man. He is a perfect man in the sense that he has reached the goal of growth; and (2) second is the idea of equipment, or being completely equipped. In other words, the details are in order. A home, for instance, can be spoken of as being fully equipped. It has everything that a home ought to have: furniture, curtains, rugs, and everything else. It is perfectly supplied or equipped. This is what Paul had in mind here.

Paul accordingly prayed that God would supply or bring to completion what was lacking in these Christians' faith so that they would be fully equipped for life and service. At this point their faith needed to be enlarged. Their lives were not complete in their spiritual experience. Paul wanted God to bring them to that further step of perfection. Nowhere in the Bible is the word *perfect* used to mean sinlessly perfect. As seen in the discussion above, the thought here is of completion or attainment, not of sinless perfection. Paul was praying that the Thessalonians might be complete and in the end might stand blameless in holiness before God.

INCREASING AND ABOUNDING IN LOVE (3:11–12)

3:11–12 Now may our God and Father himself, and our Lord Jesus, direct our way to you, and may the Lord make you increase and abound in love for one another and for all, as we do for you.

Here Paul breathed another prayer that he might have the opportunity
to see the Thessalonians again. The word "direct" refers to navigating a
straight course without frequent stops or detours. Paul was praying here for
the Lord to level and restore the road that Satan had blocked to prevent his
coming to visit the Thessalonians that was mentioned in 2:18. Paul longed to
see the Thessalonians again—and it appears that God graciously answered
this prayer about five years later when Paul visited Macedonia to encourage
the churches there (cf. Acts 20:1–3).

Verse 12 contains one of the 32 "one another" passages in the New Testament. God's people are to love one another with a love that is to be increasing and abounding. This is especially important in times of affliction and
trial when it is easy to focus on ourselves. Warren Wiersbe notes, "Times of
suffering can be times of selfishness. Persecuted people often become very
self-centered and demanding. What life does to us depends on what life finds
in us; and nothing reveals the true inner man like the furnace of affliction.
Some people build walls in times of trial, and shut themselves off. Others
build bridges and draw closer to the Lord and His people."[2] Even in their
time of persecution and trial, the Thessalonians were to shun the temptation
to become self-focused and increase in love for others. Paul prayed for them
to love one another more, and God answered this prayer (cf. 2 Thess. 1:3).

The call to increase in love is a sober reminder for us. The most dangerous thing in our spiritual experience is to ease off and to rest on our oars.
Normal Christian growth brings with it an increase in love to each other and
to all people. While the Thessalonians were a model church, there was still
room for growth and improvement in their love.

BLAMELESS IN HOLINESS (3:13)

3:13 So that he may establish your hearts blameless in holiness
before our God and Father, at the coming of our Lord Jesus with
all his saints.

The Lord's coming was mentioned again in verse 13, as it is in every chapter of the Thessalonian epistles. Chapter 1 dealt with waiting for the Lord's return (v. 10). Chapter 2 spoke of the presence of our Christ at His coming (v. 19). The last verse of chapter 3 dealt once again with the coming of the Lord. As he prayed for these Christians, Paul had in mind not only their present holiness, but also their need to go on to perfection and completion.

This verse also continued Paul's prayer that his readers may abound in love in order to be "blameless in holiness." H. A. Ironside, well-known pastor of Moody Memorial Church for eighteen years and great expositor of the Scriptures in the first half of the twentieth century, struggled in his early years with the problem of holiness. He earnestly sought an experience of complete sanctification. The story is told in his book *Holiness, the False and the True*, in which he said he thought he had to be completely holy or perfect in order to be saved.

Accordingly, Dr. Ironside would have some experience and believe he was saved and completely sanctified. He would go on for a week or two and then suddenly he would be aware that he was not perfect after all. Then he came to the conclusion that he was not saved. So he would do the whole thing over again. In this difficulty he discovered Hebrews 12:14, where he read, "Strive for peace with everyone, and for the holiness without which no one will see the Lord." He reasoned correctly that what one strives for he has not attained, but that it will be attained when he sees the Lord.

This same thought is found here in 1 Thessalonians 3:13, where Paul also mentioned holiness in connection with the Lord's coming. While we are imperfect in this life, constantly falling short and having to come to God in confession of our sins, the day is coming when we will be perfect, absolutely blameless, not only in our position before God but in our spiritual state. That day will arrive when we stand before Christ at His coming. We are rightly concerned about the imperfections in our lives; but, if He has saved us, He will never let us go until He has brought us to perfection which will be realized when Christ comes for His own. This was the great expectation behind Paul's prayer that these Thessalonians might grow in grace and attain the ultimate goal of being blameless in holiness before Christ at His coming.

Verse 13 has attracted students of the Word from another standpoint concerning the expression, "at the coming of our Lord Jesus with all his saints." Many Bible teachers, including myself, point out that the Lord is coming for His church at any time. We believe in the imminent, any-moment return of Christ, that 1 Thessalonians 4:13–18 will be fulfilled, that the dead in Christ will rise, and that living Christians will be raptured to heaven without dying into the presence of God. We further believe that after this event there will take place a great time of trouble in the world, predicted by Daniel and Christ Himself, culminating in the great tribulation. We believe that at the end of the great tribulation Christ is coming back to earth in power and glory from heaven with the saints and the holy angels, and that He will establish His righteous government on the earth, as predicted many times in the Bible. Christ's kingdom will last for one thousand years (Rev. 20:1–6) and ultimately will be followed by the eternal state after the judgment of the great white throne.

Where does this passage fit into this background? Many expositors, in considering this particular expression, "at the coming [lit., *in* the coming] of our Lord Jesus with all his saints," have distinguished His coming *for* His saints (the rapture) and His coming *with* His saints (the second coming to establish the millennial kingdom). While this is a bona fide distinction, it raises the question: "When will Christians be presented blameless in holiness before God?" If we believe that Christ is coming before the great tribulation, we will be presented blameless in holiness before God long before His second coming to set up His kingdom. If that is true, how can we explain this portion of Scripture?

The secret of it is in the word *coming*. There are at least three great words in the New Testament used to express the truth about the coming of the Lord: *epiphaneia, apokalupsis,* and *parousia.* All three of these words are used of Christ's coming for His church. They are also used of His coming to set up His kingdom on the earth. They are not technical words, then, but general words, and all of them have to do with Christ's coming. One of them (*epiphaneia*) simply speaks of His appearing, that is, that we are going to see Him. We are told also that when Christ comes to set up His kingdom on the earth every *eye* will see Him.

The word *apokalupsis* is translated "revelation," the word used for the name of the last book of the New Testament, the Revelation of Jesus Christ in the sense that His glory will be revealed. When Christ came the first time He came in humiliation. His glory was veiled except on the Mount of Transfiguration and perhaps in the garden of Gethsemane. In the latter place, when those who came to take Him asked if He was Jesus and He said "I am," they all fell before Him to the ground, apparently struck down by a momentary flash of the glory and authority of Christ. For the most part, however, His glory was veiled even after His resurrection. When He comes the second time we will see Him in His glory, and this will be a "revelation," an unveiling.

The word here in 1 Thessalonians 3:13 is the third Greek word, *parousia*, which means "presence," but is usually translated "coming." It is derived from two words: a preposition (*para*) meaning "along," and *ousia*, which is a form of the verb *to be*; hence the word means, "to be alongside of," or "to be present." While commonly translated in the Bible by the word "coming," *parousia* itself does not strictly mean coming and is used with other meanings. It means "presence" and is translated that way in 2 Corinthians 10:10 and Philippians 2:12.

What does this word *parousia* mean here in Thessalonians? When someone is coming, we also speak of his presence. For instance, a visiting preacher might be welcomed with the words, "We are happy for the coming of Pastor John Doe." What would be meant by that? How he came would not be important; the point is that he is here, and we are glad for his presence. His coming was just the means to the end. Even in English we use the term *coming* in the sense of *presence*. That is precisely the thought here. But when are we going to be in the presence of the Father?

According to Scripture, Christians will meet Christ in the air at the rapture. We will be present with Him at that moment. After we meet Him in the air, He will take us home to glory to be in the presence of the Father and the holy angels. After that we will return back to the earth with Christ. This word *coming* here may not refer specifically to the coming of Christ with His saints to the earth, but rather the coming to heaven when they will be in the presence of the Father. That is the same thought considered in 2:19, "before our Lord Jesus at his coming," literally, "before our Lord Jesus in his presence." In 3:13, the verse, translated literally, reads, "before God, even our Father *in the presence* [italics supplied] of our Lord Jesus with all his saints."

There is a coming to the earth, but there is also the coming to heaven. What an event that arrival in heaven will be! All the holy angels will be in attendance on that day. When the dead in Christ and living Christians are caught up to be with the Lord and arrive in heaven as the trophies of grace, the marvels of God's resurrection power, they will be presented as a spotless bride, as a holy people, the workmanship of Christ. At the coming of Christ with all His saints to heaven, we will be "blameless in holiness before our God and Father," but not because of any works on our part. It will be totally due to God's marvelous grace through the Lord Jesus Christ. We will stand blameless in Christ because every sin is washed away, every unholy thing once and forever removed.

SANCTIFICATION: THE WILL OF GOD (4:1–8)

4:1–8 Finally, then, brothers, we ask and urge you in the Lord Jesus, that as you received from us how you ought to walk and to please God, just as you are doing, that you do so more and more. For you know what instructions we gave you through the Lord Jesus. For this is the will of God, your sanctification: that you abstain from sexual immorality; that each one of you know how to control his own body in holiness and honor, not in the passion of lust like the Gentiles who do not know God; that no one transgress and wrong his brother in this matter, because the Lord is an avenger in all these things, as we told you beforehand and solemnly warned you. For God has not called us for impurity, but in holiness. Therefore whoever disregards this, disregards not man but God, who gives his Holy Spirit to you.

Having held before the Thessalonians the glorious prospect of the Lord's coming, Paul then discussed the great doctrine of sanctification. The word

"Finally" in verse 1 does not mean that the letter has reached its end; it means something like "in addition" or "as the rest goes" (cf. Phil. 4:1). First Thessalonians 4:1–5:9 unpacks the three great truths presented in Paul's prayer in 3:11–13 represented by the words holiness, love, and coming.

4:1–8	Holiness
4:9–12	Love
4:13–5:9	Coming

In verses 1–8 Paul discusses the great subject of personal holiness or sanctification. The word "sanctification" or "holiness," which is the same Greek word (*hagiasmos*, to be "set apart"), occurs three times (4:3, 4, 7). Verse 1 begins with an exhortation to live for Christ. Believers were always encouraged to be growing, expanding, having more. In verse 2, Paul reminded the Thessalonians that he had passed on to them the commandment to be holy.

The call to holiness gets specific in verse 3, where Paul stated, "For this is the will of God, your sanctification." Too often when people read this verse, they stop in the middle and do not note the context. Some are also inclined to read into this word *sanctification* the thought of moral perfection. That is not what Paul meant. He was saying that the Thessalonian believers were already sanctified; they had already been set apart as holy to God.

What does it mean to be sanctified? Suppose you were living in the time of Christ and wanted to make a gift to the temple in Jerusalem. You would bring your gift of gold coins and lay them on the altar. What happened to those coins? The moment they were given to God they became sanctified. They were set apart for holy use. The sanctification did not change the character of the gold coins, but it did change their use and the purpose for which they were directed. Similarly every Christian has been positionally set apart as holy to God, even though all of us fall short of perfection in everyday life.

Even a casual study of the Bible will show that holiness does not necessarily mean moral perfection. For instance, consider this expression in 2 Peter: "Holy men of God spake as they were moved by the Holy Ghost" (2:21 KJV). Peter was referring to the Old Testament writers of Scripture and to prophets who spoke the Word of God. Were those men holy? Yes, they were. The Scripture says so. Were those men perfect? Certainly not. Were Moses and David perfect? No, yet Moses wrote the Law and David wrote some of the most beautiful psalms. They were not perfect, but were nevertheless holy. God had set apart these prophets to His own holy use, guiding them to record Scripture. The Word of God as it came forth from them was inspired of God. But they were still imperfect and had to strive just as we do for holy living.

Does this mean Christians should not strive for holiness in everyday life? Certainly not. Paul said that one important aspect of the Thessalonians' sanctification was this: "that you abstain from sexual immorality." The idol worship from which some of these believers had been saved included the most abominable and immoral rites. The Thessalonian Christians, who were primarily Gentiles, had come out of that background, where immorality and religion were all mixed up. There was no holiness in pagan religion. True holiness was an entirely new idea for these Christians.

Thus for the first time they were faced with the fact that worshiping God involved a holy life. Paul had to deal with them as he did with the Corinthians and others, reminding them that as Christians their bodies were set apart as holy to God. Remember that when Paul wrote to the Thessalonians he was in the corrupt, immoral city of Corinth with its famed temple of Aphrodite and its one thousand prostitutes. In that day extramarital relations were the norm and ceremonial prostitution was ingrained in the religious rites and practices. Thessalonica was a pagan, port city where the people worshiped gods called the Cabiri that involved rites of gross immorality.[3] Christianity introduced an entirely new mind-set for those steeped in this evil lifestyle.

Sadly, not much has changed in our culture today. It is estimated that up to 80 percent of the material on the Internet is pornography. That staggers the imagination. Gene Getz summarizes the scope of the problem:

> Our world is dominated by sex. It is used in advertising to sell everything from oil to toothpaste. The displays in the window of the retail clothing store at the mall shout just one word, and it's *sex*. Entertainment features

sexual themes, sexual overtones, sexual undertone, and often just plain sex. Films and programs are labeled AC for adult content, SC for sexual content, N for nudity, PG-13, R, NC-17, and X, besides the vague listing MC for mature content. This is a sex-driven culture, one in which lust is constantly being fanned into flames. Why else would the most prominent usage of the Internet be to access pornographic Web sites?[4]

Believers are to "abstain from sexual immorality." The word "abstain" (*apechō*) means "to hold oneself off of," which is similar to Paul's statement in 1 Corinthians 6:18 "flee from immorality," and his command in 2 Timothy 2:22, "flee youthful passions." This command is beautifully illustrated in the life of Joseph (Gen. 39:6–12). Sexual immorality (*porneia*) is a broad, all-inclusive term that refers to all sexual relations outside monogamous, heterosexual marriage (fornication, adultery, homosexuality, and pornography). God's standard for sexual ethics is very simple: the only one-flesh, sexual relationship God sanctions is between a man and a woman after marriage and within marriage.

The means of obeying this instruction is "that each of you know how to control his own body in holiness and honor." The word translated "body" in the ESV is the Greek word for "vessel" (*skeuos*). There are two main views of what Paul meant.

1. Wife There are two major arguments in favor of *skeuos* meaning wife: (1) The verb *ktasthai* normally means "to get" or "acquire," which fits much better if *skeuos* refers to a wife, and (2) this meaning parallels other passages such as 1 Corinthians 6:12–7:5 and 1 Peter 3:7.

2. Body Seven points favor interpreting this phrase as meaning "control his own body in holiness and honor."

1. In the Greek papyri the verb *ktasthai* can mean "possess" or "control" in the present tense.
2. *Skeuos* always refers to one's body in the New Testament when not

taken in its literal sense (cf. Acts 9:15; Rom. 9:21–23; 2 Cor. 4:7; 2 Tim. 2:21; 1 Pet. 3:7; Rev. 2:27).

3. Being married is no guarantee of sexual purity; whereas, having one's body under control is a fail-safe formula for purity.

4. Paul is addressing men and women.

5. In the New Testament not all believers were commanded to marry but all were to keep their bodies under control.

6. To take this as referring to marriage places singleness in a negative light not seen elsewhere in the New Testament.

7. Presenting the wife as a "vessel" for the man is not a very exalted view of the marriage relationship.

The main way to abstain from sexual immorality is by self-control over one's body. In keeping with the high moral standards befitting Christians, Paul exhorted them not to give themselves to "the passion of lust like the Gentiles who do not know God." In 4:5–8 five reasons are given for abstaining from sexual immorality:

1. Abstaining from sexual immorality contrasts believers with the world (v. 5).
   Sexual purity is one of the key things that marks believers off from the world.

2. Immorality defrauds and cheats others (v. 6a).
   Verse 6 says, "that no one transgress and wrong his brother in this matter." The word "transgress" means "to go beyond, to cross a line." God has drawn a line. To go beyond that line is to go "out of bounds," to cross a forbidden frontier. God has written a sexual "No Trespassing" sign over every person who is not one's husband or wife.

3. God will judge (v. 6b).
   This judgment may come in the form or a ruined marriage, divorce, loss of family, loss of respect, trials and troubles, anxiety, or guilt. According to 1 Corinthians 6:18 sexual sin carries a built-in, self-deteriorating mechanism. Whatever the form of judgment, one

thing is for sure: you will never get away with it.

4. It is contrary to the believer's calling (v. 7).

Verse 7 says, "For God has not called us for impurity, but in holiness." Committing sexual sin goes against the whole reason you were called by Christ.

5. It is rejecting God (v. 8).

This is crystal clear in verse 8, "whoever disregards this, disregards not man but God." Engaging in sexual immorality is disregarding what God says. Sexual immorality is saying in essence, "God, Your way is not best. I know better than You what's good for me." As someone has wisely said, "You may have two consenting adults, but you don't have a consenting God."

This section concludes with the words, "God, who gives his Holy Spirit to you." Again we are reminded that our bodies are indwelt by the Spirit who empowers us. Each believer is a temple of the Holy Spirit, and therefore he is set apart as holy to God. Believers need to live in the light of this truth! Do we realize that our lives have been bought by the precious blood of Christ? Do we realize that our bodies are a holy temple occupied by the Holy Spirit? (1 Cor. 6:19–20). That is true whether we recognize it or not. Paul appealed to the Thessalonians to lead a life of holiness, being set apart to the holy things of God, free from sexual immorality.

CHRISTIAN LOVE IS HOLY (4:9–12)

4:9–12 Now concerning brotherly love you have no need for anyone to write to you, for you yourselves have been taught by God to love one another, for that indeed is what you are doing to all the brothers throughout Macedonia. But we urge you, brothers, to do this more and more, and to aspire to live quietly, and to mind your own affairs, and to work with your hands, as we instructed you, so that you may walk properly before outsiders and be dependent on no one.

The words "Now concerning" introduce a new topic. These verses focus on the subject of brotherly love (*philadelphia*). Christian love is introduced in stark contrast to pagan lust. What a difference! Paul urged the Thessalonians to love one another "more and more." Love is a growing experience. We should increase more and more in our love. Do we love the Lord Jesus Christ more today than we did a year ago, or two years ago, or three years ago? We ought to. Or are we slipping further and further away in danger of losing our first love (Rev. 2:4)? If we have been going on with the Lord we know more about Him, and the more we know about Him the more we will love Him. If we do not love the Lord Jesus, it is because we are not very well acquainted with Him. As we grow to love Him more, our love for other believers should also grow.

Paul commended his readers for their love for one another, but he also exhorted them to excel even more in love. In verses 11–12, he then gave three practical ways they could improve their love or make it more complete: (1) lead a quiet life, (2) mind their own business, and (3) be self-supporting.[5]

This is sound wisdom. Sometimes Christians get so concerned with the Lord's coming that they forget that there is a task to do right now. Paul was a very practical man. He believed in the glory to come, but he also believed that we should lead practical lives. To "live quietly" could be translated "seek restlessly to be still" or "seek earnestly to be still." Many people, especially in our modern world of cell phones, text messages, twitter, and emails, are too busy and frantic in life to have time to slow down and love others. Our culture of busyness and overload is not conducive to growing love. Stop and think about it—how often do you feel loved by an excessively busy, restless person?

The second way to improve our love is to mind our own business. No one gets into trouble minding his *own* business, but if he starts minding someone else's business, that usually causes a lot of trouble and impedes our love for others. Love is never to be confused with meddling in the lives of others.

Third, we are to work hard and be self-supporting. Honest toil is a good thing, and God's people need to work to earn an honest living. The Bible includes many illustrations of this. The prophets Haggai and Zechariah, who exhorted Israel to build the temple, recorded that the people worked with their own hands. When Paul ministered the gospel and ran out of funds, he did not wring his hands and say, "God has not been faithful to me." Oh no! He made more tents. He worked with his own hands (cf. 1 Cor. 4:12). That is perfectly honorable. Today the standard too often is to do as little as one can for as much as one can. But the Bible's standard is just the opposite.

Evidently some at Thessalonica had a problem in this area that Paul addressed later (cf. 1 Thess. 5:14; 2 Thess. 3:6–12). Perhaps their end-time fervor led to this wrong attitude. They may have been so focused on Christ's return that they did not see any need to keep working. In any event, the key is that being a parasite on other believers reveals a lack of love for them. We are not to deliberately impose on others. The purpose of this is "so that you may live properly before outsiders and be dependent on no one." In other words, pay your debts and live in such a way financially that you give a good testimony to the watching world. Sometimes Christians are not too careful in their business relationships. David Jackman provides an excellent summary of this section: "The watching world is not hugely impressed by emotional hype and extremism, but is attracted by ordinary people, living ordinary lives, who demonstrate an extraordinary godliness, seen in love."[6]

This business of sanctification, this call to holiness, extends to every aspect of our lives. We have been sanctified by the blood of Christ, by the power and presence of the Holy Spirit, by the purposes of God in our lives in time and eternity. May we give ourselves to these things as the Holy Spirit speaks to our heart.

NOTES

1. Charles R. Swindoll, *Contagious Christianity: A Study of I Thessalonians,* Bible Study Guide (Anaheim, CA: Insight for Living, 1993), 31.

2. Warren W. Wiersbe, *The Bible Exposition Commentary: An Exposition of the New Testament,* vol. 2 (Wheaton, IL: Victor, 1989), 173.

3. John Stott, *The Gospel and the End of Time: The Message of 1 & 2 Thessalonians* (Downers Grove, IL: InterVarsity, 1991), 81.

4. Gene A. Getz and Tony Beckett, *1 Thessalonians: Moving Forward in a Backward World* (Lincoln, NE: Back to the Bible, 2001), 45.

5. Ibid., 53–54.

6. David Jackman, *The Authentic Church: A Study of the Letters to the Thessalonians* (Fearn, Ross-shire, Scotland: Christian Focus, 1998), 111.

The Rapture
of the Church
1 Thessalonians 4:13–18

First Thessalonians 4 contains one of the outstanding eschatological passages in the New Testament. This section, along with John 14:1–3 and 1 Corinthians 15:50–58, is one of the key New Testament passages on the rapture of the church. A new topic is introduced in 4:13. Here the focus of the letter shifts from the present to the future resurrection of the dead and rapture of the living at the *parousia* of Christ.

As we have already noted, in this epistle there is constant reference to future things, each chapter closing with some allusion to prophecy. It was typical of the early church to have daily expectation that Christ would return. The early believers greeted one another with the word *maranatha*, "Our Lord, come!" (1 Cor. 16:22). None of the apostles or early Christians, however, realized that the church age in which we are living would be extended two thousand years. They, of course, did not set any date for the return of the Lord, but they were looking for His coming in their lifetime, and this expectation continued in the early church fathers.

The Old Testament includes many predictions on both Christ's first and second comings. Often both comings were seen in one picture. The disciples did not understand the distinction between the two comings because the Old Testament does not make clear that there was to be a period of time between the first and second comings of Christ. The disciples anticipated that when Christ came the first time He would fulfill the prophecies that pertained to His second coming, such as the earthly reign of Christ, the kingdom of righteousness and peace, and the deliverance of the Jews from their enemies, the Romans. They expected that Christ would reign and that they would reign with Him. That is why they were so disappointed and disillusioned when Christ began to tell them that it was necessary for Him to die.

They could not fit this into the picture. They thought Christ was going to bring in the messianic kingdom immediately.

In John 14:1–3, in the very shadow of the cross, Christ revealed an amazing new revelation that He had not tried to teach the disciples before—that there was another purpose of God to be fulfilled first before bringing in the millennial kingdom. Christ told the disciples:

> Let not your hearts be troubled. Believe in God; believe also in me. In my Father's house are many rooms. If it were not so, would I have told you that I go to prepare a place for you? And if I go and prepare a place for you, I will come again and will take you to myself, that where I am you may be also.

In other words, Jesus revealed to them that before He fulfilled His purpose to establish His kingdom on earth, He would come back for them and take them to dwell with Him in the Father's house in heaven before He returned to the earth. Of course, the early Christians did not completely understand this truth, just as many Christians today do not completely understand it. But it inspired a daily expectancy and eager anticipation of His return. They were looking for Christ to come and take them home to heaven. This was not death, though when a Christian dies we believe that he is "away from the body and at home with the Lord" (2 Cor. 5:8). They were looking for Christ to come and take them home to glory without dying.

John 14:1–3 is Jesus' brief introduction to the doctrine of the rapture. The full disclosure of this teaching was later committed to Paul. There are striking parallels between John 14:1–3 and 1 Thessalonians 4:13–18 that indicate they refer to the same event. J. B. Smith notes numerous linguistic similarities (see chart on the next page).[1]

Based on these comparisons, Smith observes, "The words or phrases are almost an exact parallel. They follow one another in both passages in exactly the same order. Only the righteous are dealt with in each case, there is not a single irregularity in the progression of words from first to last. Either column takes the believer from the troubles of earth to the glories of heaven."[2] When

JOHN 14:1–3		1 THESSALONIANS 4:13–18	
trouble	v. 1	sorrow	v. 13
believe	v. 1	believe	v. 14
God, me	v. 1	Jesus, God	v. 14
told you	v. 2	say to you	v. 15
come again	v. 3	coming of the Lord	v. 15
receive you	v. 3	caught up	v. 17
to myself	v. 3	to meet the Lord	v. 17
be where I am	v. 3	ever be with the Lord	v. 17

Paul wrote in 1 Thessalonians 4:15, "For this we declare to you by a word from the Lord," he may have been referring to some special revelation he received from the Lord about the rapture, but he could also have been referring back to the Lord's own words about this great event in John 14:1–3.

Though Paul had been in Thessalonica a short time, it is quite clear that he taught the Christians there this truth. This epistle makes plain that they had no doubt as to the truth that Christ was coming back for them. But there was an issue that Paul had not made clear. When Timothy brought his report to Paul, he told him about this issue that needed further clarification. The issue revolved around the *time* when their loved ones who had died in Christ would be raised. What part would Christians who have died have when the Lord returns?

It is evident that Paul had taught them that there would be a number of resurrections in a chronological order as the Scriptures portray—not just one general resurrection as some believe today. The question in their minds was: In the order of the various resurrections, when would their deceased loved ones in Christ be raised? Apparently they thought they would be caught up to be with the Lord at any time and that the resurrection of their loved ones would be delayed, possibly until after the great tribulation when Christ comes back to establish His kingdom. They wondered if those who die before the Lord's coming would miss out on this great event. They wanted some instruction on this point, so Paul wrote to answer this nagging question.

THE CERTAINTY OF CHRISTIAN HOPE (4:13–14)

4:13–14 But we do not want you to be uninformed, brothers, about those who are asleep, that you may not grieve as others do who have no hope. For since we believe that Jesus died and rose again, even so, through Jesus, God will bring with him those who have fallen asleep.

One of the great facts of the Christian faith is that we have hope when our loved ones in Christ are taken away from us in death. Christians often fail to realize the hopelessness and despair that characterizes people in pagan religions. No hope in the future life exists apart from the Lord Jesus Christ. A Christian has a wonderful hope that after this life he will have a glorious, unending existence in the presence of God, with all the joy and ecstasy that will be ours when we are united with Christ and our loved ones in Christ who have gone on before us. Paul did not want the Thessalonians to have the attitude of the pagan world that has no hope; instead he wanted them to enter experimentally into the glory of the hope that was before them.

In verse 14 the ground or basis for that hope is given. Our hope is certain because the precious truth concerning Christ's coming for His own is as certain as the central doctrines of His death and resurrection. Unless we are absolutely certain concerning the death and resurrection of Christ, we are not certain in our Christian hope. The place to begin is at the cross of Christ. There Christ died for our sins; there we had a substitute, One who was able to save us and who provided a sufficient sacrifice for our sin. We do not progress in our Christian faith until we come to the cross. Linked with the cross is Christ's resurrection, which is God's seal and the evidence or the apologetic for our Christian faith. Here is the stamp of certainty: Christ rose from the dead. One way to think of this is that Christ's death is the full payment for our sins, and His resurrection is the receipt for that payment (cf. Rom. 4:25). It is proof that God accepted Christ's perfect sacrifice on our behalf. If we believe that Christ died for us and rose from the dead, and really believe it by receiving Jesus Christ as our Savior, then we have a ground for hope that we too will be raised.

One reason so many people these days do not consider seriously the coming of Christ for them is that they have not been at His cross enough. Pulpits that do not proclaim the death of Christ and His resurrection can hardly be expected to preach the coming of the Lord. All these events are tied together. If we accept what the Scriptures teach about the first coming of Christ and put our trust in Him, then there will be planted in our hearts an earnest desire to see the Savior, and the truth of His coming for us will be exceedingly precious. Do we really anticipate the Lord's appearing? Does it mean anything that Christ might come back today? Many Christians may believe in His return as a part of their doctrinal beliefs, but they may not have this as their daily expectation. This may be part of their creed but not part of their continual anticipation. The difficulty is that their hearts and minds are not really fixed on Christ. They hold to the truth of the Lord's coming, but the truth does not hold them. We will love the appearing of the Lord in direct proportion to our love for the Lord Himself. If we love Him, if we long to see Him who first loved us, then the truth of the Lord's coming and the fact that He could come today will be a precious truth.

Verse 13 refers to "those who are asleep," and verses 14 and 15 repeat the phrase "those who have fallen asleep." Sleep is a softened expression or euphemism for death, which for a Christian is very much like sleep (Matt. 27:52; John 11:11; Acts 7:60). The word "sleep" (*koimaomai*) was used in the early church of a corpse since it looks like it is asleep and will be awakened at the resurrection. We get our word "cemetery" from the Greek word *koimeterion*. As John Stott says, "Cemeteries are dormitories for the dead."[3]

We understand from Scripture that "sleep" refers to bodies that are laid in the grave. But our souls and spirits go immediately into God's presence and the conscious enjoyment of heaven, for to be "away from the body" is to be "at home with the Lord" (2 Cor. 5:8), as noted above. Paul also described a believer's death as "to depart and be with Christ" (Phil. 1:23). We believe in the sleep of the body, but we do not believe in a teaching often called "soul sleep," which says that the soul is unconscious during the interim period between death and the Lord's coming. The soul or immaterial part of a believer goes immediately to be with the Lord. The body sleeps in the grave, but will be resurrected when Christ comes back.

A problem exists in verse 14 in the statement, "through Jesus, God will bring with him those who have fallen asleep." Some translations connect the words "through Jesus" with "those who have fallen asleep." This carries the idea that believers fall asleep or die "through Jesus." But what does it mean to sleep "through Jesus"? The meaning is that when a Christian dies, his hope of being in the presence of God is made possible through Jesus. Our loved ones who are asleep through Jesus go to sleep in the certain hope of waking. Other translations, such as the ESV, take the expression "through Jesus" to go with "God will bring with him." This is also true and could be the meaning of the expression. Either way, all of our hope in living and in dying is certainly "through Jesus" (cf. 1 Cor. 8:6).

THE TIME OF THE RESURRECTION (4:15–18)

4:15 For this we declare to you by a word from the Lord, that we who are alive, who are left until the coming of the Lord, will not precede those who have fallen asleep.

In verse 15 and following Paul answered the Thessalonians' main question. They did not ask, "Is the Lord coming?" or "Will we be with the Lord?" They believed this. The central question was, "What will happen to our loved ones who have preceded us in death?" Some of the Thessalonians may have died a martyr's death. In any case, in the few months since Paul had been in Thessalonica apparently some of the believers had died. This reminds us of the uncertainty of life. Whether we are young or old, whether well or in poor health, we do not know how much time God will give us to serve Him in this world. Those in the Thessalonian church who had already died in Christ were illustrations of the uncertainty of human life. We should be living every day in such a way that if it is our last day on earth, it will have been a day well spent in the Master's will. We must count our days so that we make sure our days count (Ps. 90:12; Eph. 5:16).

The question had been also asked: "When will the dead in Christ be raised?" Paul gave the answer in verse 16: "The dead in Christ will rise first," followed by the living (v. 17). Both groups will be "caught up together," or raptured, to be with Christ. This passage teaches that when Christ returns He will come back to the atmospheric heaven. When that and the other events pictured here occur, Christians whose bodies have been in the grave will be resurrected, their bodies will be transformed into resurrection bodies, and they will meet the Lord in the air. All of this will take place in a split second. Then living Christians will be translated from their bodies of flesh into resurrected, immortal, imperishable, incorruptible bodies.

The companion passage to 1 Thessalonians 4 is the revelation given in 1 Corinthians 15:50–53. Just as the former passage teaches about the dead in Christ, so the latter teaches about the translation of the living saints. First Corinthians 15:50–53 reads:

I tell you this, brothers: flesh and blood cannot inherit the kingdom of God, nor does the perishable inherit the imperishable. Behold! I tell you a mystery. We shall not all sleep, but we shall all be changed, in a moment, in the twinkling of an eye, at the last trumpet. For the trumpet will sound, and the dead will be raised imperishable, and we shall be changed. For this perishable body must put on the imperishable, and this mortal body must put on immortality.

Here the *order* of the resurrection of Christians is taught very plainly. Christians who have died will be resurrected just a moment before the rapture of living saints. The word "moment" is the Greek word *atomōs*, which refers to something that cannot be cut or divided any further, something that is indivisible. The speed with which these events occur is also described as "in the twinkling of an eye." While some maintain that this refers to the time it takes for light to gleam off a human eye, it probably is a reference to the time it takes to blink, the fastest movement of the human body.

Those rising from the grave and living believers on the earth will be caught up to meet the Lord in the air. The Scriptures make it clear that when Christ comes for His own He will take them to heaven, where He has gone now to prepare a place for us in the Father's house (John 14:1–3). Following the rapture the church will be in glory, but on earth the great climactic event of this age, the great tribulation, will rage. Yet even during that awful time the Lord will graciously call many Jews and Gentiles to trust in Christ (Rev. 7:1–18). Many will be martyred in this period. The climax will come when Christ returns in power and glory with the angels and with the church from heaven to set up His righteous kingdom on the earth.

FIVE PRINCIPAL VIEWS ON THE TIMING OF THE RAPTURE

One of the key issues concerning the rapture of the church is the timing of this event in relation to the tribulation. There are five principal views today regarding the timing of the rapture. Here is a brief description of each view:

Pretribulation Rapture

Pretribulationalism, which is the position of this commentary, teaches that the rapture of the church will occur before the commencement of the seven-year tribulation period. The church will not be present on earth during any part of this outpouring of God's wrath. At some point after the rapture the tribulation will begin when the Antichrist enters into a seven-year treaty or covenant with Israel (Dan. 9:27).

Midtribulation Rapture

The midtribulational view is that Christ will rapture His church at the mid-point of the tribulation. Believers will have to endure the first half of the seven-year tribulation. Midtribulationists maintain that the last half of the tribulation is the time when God will pour out His wrath on the world. Believers will be caught up to heaven before this time of wrath. Midtribu-lationists defend their view by noting the frequent mention of three and a half years (42 months or 1,260 days) in Daniel and Revelation. But the main argument of midtribulationists is their equating the last trumpet in 1 Corinthians 15:52 with the seventh trumpet in Revelation 11:15. One of the key problems with this view is that midtribulationalists cannot even agree among themselves on where to place the rapture in the book of Revelation. Some say the rapture is predicted in Revelation 6:12–17; others say 11:15–17; and others suggest 14:1–4.

Posttribulation Rapture

Posttribulationism holds that the rapture will occur at the end of the tribu-lation immediately before the second coming of Christ back to earth. Believers will be raptured up to meet Christ in the air and then will return immediately with Him back to the earth. The rapture and second coming are basically viewed as one event separated by a few moments. Posttribu-lationalists usually argue that while church-age believers will be present on earth during the tribulation, God will protect them from the outpouring of His wrath.

Partial Rapture

The partial-rapture position distinguishes between devout believers and worldly believers. According to this view, faithful, devoted believers who are looking for Christ's coming will be raptured to heaven before the tribulation.

This view is based on New Testament passages that stress obedient watching and waiting for Christ (Matt. 25:1–13; 1 Thess. 5:6; Heb. 9:28; 1 John 2:28). Other believers will enter the tribulation and be caught up during subsequent raptures throughout the tribulation. One writer described the partial rapture view like this: "All believers will go home on the same train, but not all on the first section."[4] While there are several problems with this view, the main one is that the Bible uses all-inclusive words such as "we" and "all" when discussing the rapture. This indicates that all believers will be raptured at the same time. "*We* shall not *all* sleep, but *we* shall *all* be changed" (1 Cor. 15:51b, italics added). First Thessalonians 4:14b says that when Christ comes He will bring with Him *all* "those who have fallen asleep." The only qualification for participating in the rapture according to 1 Thessalonians 4:16 is that a person be "in Christ." In other words, all a person must do is be a Christian. No other requirement is stated.

Pre-wrath Rapture

The pre-wrath rapture view states that the rapture will occur about three-fourths, or five and a half years, of the way through the tribulation. According to this view the catastrophes in the first three-fourths of the tribulation will result from the wrath of man and the wrath of Satan, not the wrath of God. God's wrath will not be poured out until the seventh seal in Revelation. Believers will be taken up just before the wrath of God begins to be poured out on the earth. This is a more obscure view compared to the other four.

These views (except partial rapture) are presented in the chart on the next page.

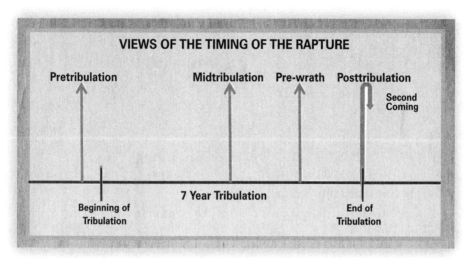

4:16–17 For the Lord himself will descend from heaven with a cry of command, with the voice of an archangel, and with the sound of the trumpet of God. And the dead in Christ will rise first. Then we who are alive, who are left, will be caught up together with them in the clouds to meet the Lord in the air, and so we will always be with the Lord.

Other aspects of this revelation deserve closer study. Verse 16 states that the Lord Himself will descend from heaven with a shout or "cry of command," a word describing the shout of a military officer giving a command such as "Forward, march!" We see an example of Christ's shout of command in John 11:43 at the tomb of Lazarus. When Christ said, "Lazarus, come out," Lazarus arose and came out of his tomb. Some have commented that if Christ had left off the name of Lazarus, all the dead would have come forth! Such is the authority and sovereignty of the Lord Jesus Christ. Lazarus was not resurrected in the sense that we will be. He was restored to a mortal body and in due time, as age came on him, he no doubt died a natural death and was returned to the tomb. But Christians will be resurrected like Christ, with a resurrection body like His which will never wear out or be subject to death, disease, or pain—a body that will last for all eternity, suited for the glorious presence of the Lord. The new, glorified body of the believer is vividly described in 1 Corinthians 15:35–49.

Along with the "cry of command" from Jesus will be "the voice of an archangel," who is none other than Michael, the chief of the angels (Dan. 12:1; Jude 9), and the special protector of Israel. He too will give a shout. The Bible does not explain why Michael will give this shout or why he should be included. The Scriptures do reveal, however, that a great battle of the ages is going on, a battle that began in the garden of Eden and perhaps even before, and has continued through the present age.

This cosmic battle is against the forces of darkness, the forces of Satan, and the evil angels and demons who are associated with him. This is why Paul tells us that our battle is not "against flesh and blood" (Eph. 6:12). This is why we need to pray without ceasing (1 Thess. 5:17); why we need to come to God for protection, care, and guidance; and why we need to put on the whole armor of God (Eph. 6:11). The archangel's shout is a shout of victory not only for believers, but a shout of victory for the angels. Even though the rapture is a work of Christ and not the angels, the archangel will rejoice and exult in the tremendous victory over the forces of evil that will be won when the church is resurrected from the dead.

Another significant expression is "the trumpet of God." This is a third great sound that will accompany and signal the Lord's coming. Many trumpets are mentioned in Scripture. In the Old Testament trumpets were sounded at the beginning of each month (Num. 10:10); and the feast of trumpets was on the first day of the month (Lev. 23:24; Num. 29:1); and on countless other occasions trumpets were blown. In the marching order when Israel moved about in the wilderness, trumpets were used. In Scripture the trumpet seems to be a sign of assembling, a sign of going forward, of taking a new step, of unfolding something that has not been revealed before. The sounding of the trumpet here is like the sounding of the trumpet to an army. This is a call to march forward. So in 1 Thessalonians 4:16 there is the shout, the voice of the archangel, and the trumpet of God. These are three separate things, but they picture one grand event: the coming of Christ for His church, and the rapture of the living believers and the resurrection of the dead from scenes of earth to scenes of heaven. As Hiebert notes, "Clearly the rapture does not seem to be a silent affair. It seems that a tremendous reverberating sound will actually encircle the earth."[5]

Some students of Scripture have had difficulty with the trumpet of God in this verse because they find other trumpets in the Bible. For instance, the book of Revelation mentions seven trumpets (Rev. 8:5–9:21; 11:15–19). These are part of the dramatic sequence of events unfolded in what Christ called the great tribulation. Revelation first presents seven seals. Out of the seventh seal there comes a series of events called the seven trumpets, and out of the seventh trumpet comes another series of events known as the seven bowls of God's wrath. These picture in very graphic language the climactic events of the great tribulation leading up to the second coming of Christ.

First Corinthians 15:52 mentions "the last trumpet" in conjunction with the rapture. Based on this some have said that if this is the last trumpet, it must be the seventh trumpet of Revelation. That certainly is not true! Actually the last trumpet of Revelation is not the last trumpet in the Bible at all. At Christ's second coming, which will occur after the seven bowls of wrath, another trumpet will be sounded (Matt. 24:31) that will call the elect of God together.

Is this trumpet of 1 Thessalonians 4:16 and 1 Corinthians 15:52 the same as the seventh trumpet of the Revelation? What do the seven trumpets of Revelation do? Every one of them is a judgment of God upon a Christ-rejecting world. They assemble no one; they are not symbols of salvation or deliverance, and there are no resurrections. These trumpets are symbols of judgment upon those living in the world who have rejected the Lord Jesus Christ.

By contrast, the trumpet of 1 Thessalonians 4:16 is a call addressed to the saved, to those who have trusted in the Lord Jesus Christ. This trumpet is one of deliverance, of grace, and of mercy. In this trumpet God will be dealing with only His saints; this trumpet has absolutely no connection with judgment on unbelievers. The only similarity is that in both cases there are trumpets. Mention of the last trumpet in 1 Corinthians 15:52 does not mean that it is the last trumpet in God's whole program. The last trumpet for the church will occur long before any of the trumpets in the book of Revelation.

77

DISTINCTION BETWEEN THE TRUMPETS
IN 1 CORINTHIANS 15 AND REVELATION 11

	LAST TRUMPET IN 1 CORINTHIANS 15:52	SEVENTH TRUMPET IN REVELATION 11:15–19
Subject:	The church	The wicked world
Nature:	Grace	Judgment
Result:	Catching up of the church	Further judgment on the world

Others try to connect the last trumpet in 1 Corinthians 15:52 with the trumpet in Matthew 24:31 and use this to support a posttribulational rapture. Hiebert provides an excellent refutation of connecting these two trumpets:

> There is a similarity between the two, since in both the blowing of the trumpet is associated with a gathering of the Lord's people; but there are marked differences. The subjects are different: here [in 1 Cor. 15:52] the reference is to the church; there [in Matt. 24:31] the Olivet Discourse portrays Jewish believers during the Great tribulation. The circumstances are different: here the trumpet is connected with the raising of the believing dead; there no mention is made of a resurrection, but it is connected with a regathering of the elect who have been scattered over the earth. The result is different: here the blowing of the trumpet results in the uniting of the raised dead with the living as one body to be caught up to meet the Lord in the air; there the elect are the living believers who are regathered from all parts of the earth at the command of their Lord who has returned to earth in open glory.[6]

First Thessalonians 4 continues with another tremendous revelation: "And the dead in Christ will rise first. Then we who are alive, who are left, will be caught up together with them in the clouds to meet the Lord in the air, and

DISTINCTION BETWEEN THE TRUMPETS IN 1 CORINTHIANS 15 AND MATTHEW 24		
	LAST TRUMPET IN 1 CORINTHIANS 15:52	TRUMPET IN MATTHEW 24:31
Subject:	The church	The Jews in the tribulation
Circumstance:	Raising the dead	Regathering the elect
Result:	United with the Lord in the air	Gathered on earth

so we will always be with the Lord" (vv. 16b–17). This Scripture does not reveal where we are to go with the Lord. Posttribulationalists, who view the rapture and the second coming as simultaneous events, maintain that the saints will be caught up to meet Christ in the air and then turn around and escort Him immediately back to earth at His second coming. Support for this view is often based on the word "meet" (*apantēsin*). Posttribulationalists argue that this word carries a technical meaning of a group of people going out of a city to meet a dignitary and ceremonially escorting the person back to the city. However, the best-known, most trusted Greek lexicon today simply gives the meaning of the word as "to meet" without any mention of the idea of returning back to the starting point.[7] The only other place in the New Testament where this word is used is Acts 28:15, which speaks of believers going to "the Forum of Appia and Three Taverns to meet [*apantēsin*]" Paul. But again the word simply means "to meet," not "to meet and escort back." The posttribulational timing of the rapture is not supported by this term.

If we want to discover where believers will go after meeting Christ in the air, we can look to the parallel passage in John 14:1–3. There Jesus states plainly that when He comes for His own, He will take us to the Father's house in heaven. When we meet the Lord in the air, we shall assemble in the atmospheric heaven and from there go to the third heaven, which is the immediate presence of the Father. This is further supported in the last part of the preceding chapter where Paul spoke of our being "blameless in holiness before our God and Father, at the coming of our Lord Jesus with all his saints" (3:13).

This will be a wonderful event when we who have trusted in Christ in this life stand in His presence. In that triumphant moment we will be like Christ, for we are told in 1 John 3:2 that we will be perfectly holy: "Beloved, we are God's children now, and what we will be has not yet appeared; but we know that when he appears we shall be like him, because we shall see him as he is." We will be cleansed from every spot and wrinkle and every sign of age, disease, and corruption. We will be a perfect and a beautiful bride for our Lord and Savior Jesus Christ, and we will be with Him forever. Whether Christ is in heaven or reigning on the earth, or in the new earth or the new heavens in eternity future, wherever He is the church will be there also. We will be with the Lord forever.

A fascinating sideline study is the expression "the dead in Christ" (v. 16). These are the ones who trusted Christ as Savior in this life and then died a physical death. Their bodies have been laid in the grave and their spirits have gone to heaven. This expression occurs about forty times in the New Testament, and in most of these instances it refers to our position in Christ. When a person receives Jesus Christ as his Savior, as the one who died for him on the cross and who shed His blood for his sins and rose in triumph, God does something. He saves his soul.

At the very moment God saves us many wonderful things happen. Dr. Lewis Sperry Chafer, the late founder of Dallas Theological Seminary, wrote a book called *Salvation* in which he listed thirty-three things that occur instantaneously the very moment a person places his trust in Jesus Christ as his Savior. For example, we are placed in Christ, meaning that we are baptized into one body and are baptized into Christ (cf. 1 Cor. 12:13). We become an integral part of the living, vital organism that is the church of Jesus Christ in the world. This occurs the instant we trust in Christ. Every genuine Christian is equally in Christ.

First Thessalonians 4 teaches that the dead in Christ will be raised when Christ comes back. It is a selective resurrection. Not all the dead will be raised.

The Scriptures make it plain that unsaved people will not be raised until many years later after the predicted millennial (one thousand year) reign of Christ. Then unbelievers will be resurrected and gathered at the great white throne judgment (Rev. 20:11–15). The question which has bothered Bible students is whether the "dead in Christ" include all the saints who have died up to this point, or whether this expression includes only the saints of this dispensation, which is commonly called the "church age," the period from the day of Pentecost until the rapture.

C. I. Scofield, who edited the *Scofield Reference Bible* that has been used by generations of Bible students, said in a note on 1 Thessalonians 4:16 that the dead in Christ includes all the saints. Dr. Chafer, who was Scofield's associate for nearly two decades, came to a different conclusion after studying the question for many years. Chafer believed that the "dead in Christ" refers only to the saints of this dispensation. If the rapture occurs *before* the time of great tribulation pictured in the Bible, then the resurrection of the Old Testament saints would occur *after* the tribulation in connection with Christ's return to establish His kingdom. If two men of God like Scofield and Chafer differ, how can we determine the correct interpretation? The key seems to be in the phrase "in Christ."

In every one of its many instances in the New Testament, the expression "in Christ" refers only to the saints of this dispensation. As far as the expression "the dead in Christ" indicates, only those in Christ are raised. Of course, all saints are in Christ in the sense that Christ is their substitute. But the question is whether they are baptized into His body, the church, as revealed in 1 Corinthians 12:13, which says, "For in one Spirit we were all baptized into one body—Jews or Greeks, slaves or free—and all were made to drink of one Spirit."

The doctrine of the resurrection of Old Testament saints, as revealed in the Old Testament itself, relates the event to Christ's second coming to establish His kingdom. By way of illustration, Daniel 12:1 deals with the great tribulation, while 12:2 speaks of many being raised from the dust of the earth. If that is a genuine resurrection, it is a clear indication that according to Daniel, the resurrection of Old Testament saints occurs after the tribulation.

The resurrection of the church, however, occurs before the tribulation. There is no explicit teaching anywhere in the Bible that reveals that the Old Testament saints are resurrected at the time the church is resurrected. The two events are never brought together in any passage of Scripture. The best explanation of the expression "dead in Christ" is that it refers to the church alone.

4:18 Therefore encourage one another with these words.

The Thessalonians were having a difficult time, and this wonderful truth of the Lord's coming, the resurrection of their loved ones, and their being gathered together to be with the Lord was a joyous prospect. This is another good reason the Lord will come for His church before the tribulation. Paul did not tell these Christians, "Now if you endure through the tribulation time, if you survive that awful period, then you will see your loved ones at the end." That would not have been an encouragement to them. That would be a blasted hope rather than a blessed hope. They were in trouble already and no doubt had been taught that the time of great tribulation would be much worse than the trouble they already had. Instead, Paul lifted up their eyes to contemplate Christ's coming, and they were encouraged by the fact that the Lord would come at any time to receive them to Himself.

This very precious truth of Christ's return is most significant, but it depends on our personal relationship to Him. Are we really trusting Him? Is our heart, our faith, our life really centered in the Lord Jesus Christ? Some Christians are actually afraid of the doctrine of the Lord's coming, and of the thought that the Lord might come today. Such an attitude is born of ignorance and unbelief. But think of the joy of looking forward to the Lord's coming and resting in these precious truths! Many ills of life can be healed only by the Lord's return. We all have loved ones on the other side. And the many problems of this life—incurable diseases, pain, sorrow, and difficulties of all kinds—will be made all right. We can face the trials and challenges of life because God has given us this blessed hope of the Lord's return. May we take it to heart, live in its reality, and be refreshed by this truth. This hope can be certain for anyone who will trust in Jesus Christ the Son of God, who loved us and died for us, who shed His blood that we might be saved, and who rose in victory that we might have hope.

NOTES

1. J. B. Smith, *A Revelation of Jesus Christ: A Commentary on the Book of Revelation* (Scottsdale, PA: Herald, 1961), 312.

2. Ibid., 313.

3. John Stott, *The Gospel and the End of Time: The Message of 1 and 2 Thessalonians* (Downers Grove, IL: InterVarsity, 1991), 96.

4. Gerald B. Stanton, *Kept from the Hour* (Miami Springs, FL: Schoettle, 1991), 166.

5. D. Edmond Hiebert, *1 and 2 Thessalonians* (Chicago: Moody, 1971), 212.

6. Ibid., 213.

7. Walter Bauer, William F. Arndt, and F. Wilbur Gingrich, *A Greek-English Lexicon of the New Testament and Other Early Christian Literature,* 3rd ed., rev. Frederick W. Danker (Chicago: University of Chicago Press, 2000), 97.

The Day of the Lord
1 Thessalonians 5:1–11

In passages like 1 Thessalonians 5:1–11, the Bible indicates that tremendous events are ahead for the world. Gathered under the expression "the day of the Lord" is a large group of prophetic events predicted in both the Old and the New Testaments. The subject of the rapture of the church revealed in 1 Thessalonians 4:13–18, however, is never mentioned in the Old Testament. There is no reference in the Old Testament to saints being raptured, that is, taken from earth to heaven without dying. That is what Paul means in 1 Corinthians 15:52 when he calls this event a "mystery." In the New Testament a mystery is not what we often think about in a book or a movie where there is a series of events to solve and untangle. A mystery in Scripture is a truth that has never been fully revealed before and that humans could never figure out on their own apart from divine revelation (Eph. 3:4–5, 9; Col. 1:26). The idea of an entire generation of believers escaping physical death was unknown in the Old Testament. It was a mystery. There are many references to Christ coming back to the earth and of resurrection from the dead, but no rapture in the Old Testament, except by way of illustration in the cases of Elijah and Enoch.

THE SUDDENNESS OF THAT DAY (5:1–3)

5:1–3 Now concerning the times and the seasons, brothers, you have no need to have anything written to you. For you yourselves are fully aware that the day of the Lord will come like a thief in the night. While people are saying, "There is peace and security," then sudden destruction will come upon them as labor pains come upon a pregnant woman, and they will not escape.

A consideration of the day of the Lord immediately plunges us into a tremendous doctrine that covers many pages in the Old Testament. Before examining the scriptural revelation, it is necessary to determine precisely what "the day of the Lord" means. We say that the present age is the day of grace. We do not mean that God showed no grace in the previous dispensations. Obviously, many of God's dealings with mankind from the garden of Eden down to the present day have manifested His grace. The salvation of every person, no matter when they lived, is a work of God's sovereign grace. But God in this present age has especially singled out the doctrine of grace for unique display, highlighting grace as the basis for salvation and for our Christian life. Grace speaks of God's unmerited favor to us through Christ, who loved us and who died for us. After this day of grace has come to its close, which may be simultaneous with the rapture of the church, the day of the Lord will begin.

The day of the Lord is a period of time in which God will deal with evil people *directly* and *dramatically* in fearful judgment. A person may be a blasphemer of God, an angry atheist, or one who openly denounces God and teaches bad doctrine. Seemingly God does nothing about it. But the day designated in Scripture as "the day of the Lord" is coming when God will punish human sin, and He will deal directly and dramatically in wrath and in judgment with a Christ-rejecting world. One thing we are sure of is that God in His own way will bring every soul into judgment.

The word *day* is used in the Bible in various ways. Sometimes it is used to refer to daylight, for instance, the hours between dawn and sunset (Gen. 1:5). Sometimes it is used to refer to a twenty-four-hour day. The Jewish day began at sunset and continued to the next day at sunset. That also is referred to as a day (Gen. 1:5). Sometimes the word *day* is used in the Bible as a period of time (Gen. 2:4), just as we use it in English. We speak of the day of our youth. We do not mean that we were young only one day, but we mean the extended period of time in which we were young.

In 1 Thessalonians 5, the day of the Lord is used in this sense of an extended period of time, but having the characteristics of a twenty-four-hour day. That is, it is a day that begins at midnight or in the darkness, advances to dawn, and then to daylight. It will close again with another period of darkness after daylight has passed. That apparently is the symbolism involved in the day of the Lord. A few sample passages, out of the nineteen references to the day of the Lord in the Old Testament, will give the general idea of this period. One such passage is Isaiah 13:9–11:

> Behold, the day of the LORD comes, cruel, with wrath and fierce anger, to make the land a desolation and to destroy its sinners from it. For the stars of the heavens and their constellations will not give their light; the sun will be dark at its rising, and the moon will not shed its light. I will punish the world for its evil, and the wicked for their iniquity; I will put an end to the pomp of the arrogant, and lay low the pompous pride of the ruthless.

This text reveals that a dramatic judgment will be manifest in the physical world, which will interfere with the light of the sun, moon, and stars. God will put down the proud and deal with sinners in judgment. The same thought is found in Zephaniah 1:14–16:

> The great day of the LORD is near, near and hastening fast; the sound of the day of the LORD is bitter; the mighty man cries aloud there. A day of wrath is that day, a day of distress and anguish, a day of ruin and devastation, a day of darkness and gloom, a day of clouds and thick darkness, a day of trumpet blast and battle cry against the fortified cities and against the lofty battlements.

This passage continues in the same strain. The day of the Lord, according to the Old Testament, is a time of God's judgment on the world in its sin.

The day of the Lord, however, is also portrayed in Scripture as a time of deliverance and blessing for Israel. The millennium—the kingdom reign of Christ on earth—in which Christ will personally direct the government of the world, is also included in the day of the Lord. In Zephaniah 3:14–17, by way of illustration, there is a picture of Israel's blessing in that day, obviously following the time of judgment:

Sing aloud, O daughter of Zion; shout, O Israel! Rejoice and exult with all your heart, O daughter of Jerusalem! The LORD has taken away the judgments against you; he has cleared away your enemies. The King of Israel, the LORD, is in your midst; you shall never again fear evil. On that day it shall be said to Jerusalem: "Fear not, O Zion; let not your hands grow weak. The LORD your God is in your midst, a mighty one who will save; he will rejoice over you with gladness; he will quiet you by his love; he will exult over you with loud singing."

This passage reveals that Israel will praise the Lord in the millennium. Another text that sheds light on the blessing phase of the day of the Lord is Joel 3. In verse 14 the "day of the Lord" is mentioned specifically. Then, while still referring to the day of the Lord, Joel says, "And in that day [the day of the Lord] the mountains shall drip sweet wine, and the hills shall flow with milk, and all the streambeds in Judah shall flow with water; and a fountain shall come forth from the house of the LORD and water the Valley of Shittim" (v. 18). The day of the Lord extends all the way into the millennial, messianic kingdom.

THE DAY OF THE LORD
IN THE OLD TESTAMENT

The Old Testament has nineteen references to the day of the Lord, but in dozens of other places it is called "the day" or "that day." Here are the specific occurrences in the Old Testament.

- Isaiah 2:12; 13:6, 9
- Ezekiel 13:5; 30:3
- Joel 1:15; 2:1, 11, 31; 3:14
- Amos 5:18 [*twice*], 20
- Obadiah 1:5
- Zephaniah 1:7, 14 [*twice*]
- Zechariah 14:1
- Malachi 4:5

Putting these passages together, the day of the Lord is any time God intervenes directly and dramatically in history either to judge or to bless. As revealed in the Old Testament, it is a period of time that will begin with the seven-year tribulation, which could be called the *judgment phase*, and will continue throughout the entire thousand-year reign of Christ, which could be called the *blessing phase*. The day of the Lord will stretch all the way from the rapture to the end of the millennium. It will commence with a time of wrath and judgment on a wicked and Christ-rejecting world and will culminate in a time of peace and prosperity in which Christ will be in the midst of the earth and will rule over the earth and bring blessing to the nation Israel. The millennium will end with another night of judgment (Rev. 20:9–15).

TWO PHASES OF THE FUTURE DAY OF THE LORD

PHASE 1—JUDGMENT	PHASE 2—BLESSING
Tribulation	Millennium
Darkness	Light
7 years	1,000 years

THE DAY OF THE LORD IN THE NEW TESTAMENT

The day of the Lord is mentioned four times in the New Testament:

- Acts 2:20
- 1 Thessalonians 5:2
- 2 Thessalonians 2:2
- 2 Peter 3:10

The truth concerning the coming of Christ for His church is revealed in 1 Thessalonians 4. The question that is answered in 1 Thessalonians 5 is, What is the relationship of the coming of Christ to the day of the Lord?

So Paul said accordingly: "Now concerning the times and the seasons, brothers, you have no need to have anything written to you." The word "times" here is a translation of the Greek word from which we get our word *chronology*. Paul referred to a general chronology, "times," and the particular chronology, "seasons." The Thessalonians had already been instructed, first, concerning the general time when Christ would come and, second, concerning the particular time. In a word, the instruction is this: The general time can be known, but the particular time cannot. There is no need to focus on the particular time because no one, including Paul, can know it, just as Jesus taught in Matthew 24:36 and Acts 1:7.

Paul continued in 1 Thessalonians 5:2–3 to describe the day of the Lord as both a "thief in the night" and as a painful time similar to a woman laboring to give birth. This day is also described as a day of wrath (v. 9), which is very important. Compare this passage with the sixth chapter of Revelation, which concerns the beginning of the great tribulation. Verses 12–14 state:

When he opened the sixth seal, I looked, and behold, there was a great earthquake, and the sun became black as sackcloth, the full moon became like blood, and the stars of the sky fell to the earth as the fig tree sheds its winter fruit when shaken by a gale. The sky vanished like a scroll that is being rolled up, and every mountain and island was removed from its place.

This is the same thought and is also a warning of judgment on men. In Revelation 6:16–17, we learn that evil people cry out and are "calling to the mountains and rocks, 'Fall on us and hide us from the face of him who is seated on the throne, and from the wrath of the Lamb, for the great day of their wrath has come, and who can stand?'" Isaiah said it is a day of wrath; Zephaniah said it is a day of wrath; Revelation 6 says it is a day of wrath. In other words, the picture we have here of the great tribulation—the time of trouble on the earth—is identical to the picture of the Old Testament revelation of the beginning of the day of the Lord.

The question is: How does the coming of Christ for His church (the rapture) relate to the day of the Lord that will precede His second coming by a number of years? This day of the Lord will come suddenly and unexpectedly. The point is that just as the translation of the church is the end of the day of grace, it also marks the beginning of the day of the Lord. In other words, the one event seems to do two things: it serves as the closing of one day and the beginning of the other.

If that is true, it gives us some very positive and definite teaching that the church will be taken out of the world before the day of trial and trouble overtakes the world. Paul was telling the Thessalonians that the day of the Lord will come, and this follows immediately after the passage on the coming of Christ for His church. The order here is instructive. The rapture is described first in 1 Thessalonians 4:13–18, and then the day of the Lord follows. First Thessalonians 5:2–3 reveals that the day of the Lord will come suddenly and unexpectedly.

The judgment will come when the world is unguarded: "There is peace and security" (v. 3)—just the opposite of the time of trouble which is predicted. Apparently the world situation at the beginning of the day of the Lord will provide a false basis for peace. This may be accomplished by a strengthened United Nations or other world organization. It will probably be the time of temporary peace forged by the coming Antichrist (Dan. 9:27; Rev. 6:1–2). He will launch his career as a great peacemaker, but eventually the mask will come off and his ruthless, selfish ambitions will be revealed.

This state of peace is in stark contrast, however, to the global scenario at the second coming. Then the armies of the world will be drawn in battle array at Armageddon. The world will be engaged in a gigantic military struggle then. But the day of the Lord will begin in a time of seeming peace. Then without any warning a time of sudden destruction will come. In 1 Thessalonians 5:3 the Greek word for *sudden* is emphasized. This event will not be preceded by signs; that is, there will be no warning. There will be no possibility of escape.

The gripping illustration given is that of labor pains coming suddenly on a pregnant woman. Just as birth pains are inescapable, and increase in intensity and frequency, so the wrath of God will pour forth in crashing waves on the earth. It will be God's inescapable, irreversible judgment on those who are "in darkness" (1 Thess. 5:4). The beginning of the day of the Lord is clearly not the second coming of Christ. It commences long before, and may begin at once or at least very soon after the day of grace closes with the rapture of the church.

SEVEN FEATURES OF THE COMING OF THE DAY OF THE LORD

Secretly	"like a thief in the night"
Unexpectedly	"while people are saying 'there is peace and security'"
Suddenly	"sudden"
Destructively	"destruction"
Inevitably	"as labor pains come upon a woman"
Irreversibly	"as labor pains come upon a woman"
Inescapably	"they will not escape"

CHRISTIANS WILL NOT BE OVERTAKEN (5:4–5)

5:4–5 But you are not in darkness, brothers, for that day to surprise you like a thief. For you are all children of light, children of the day. We are not of the night or of the darkness.

Notice the clear contrast for Christians—"but you." Christians do not know when the day of the Lord is coming either. As far as expectation is concerned, they are in the dark about it. Christ could come today and the day of the Lord would follow, but no one can set the day. It is unexpected in this sense for us. So what did Paul mean by the statement, "You are not in the darkness . . . for that day to surprise you like a thief"?

The best explanation is that we will not be here. When the day of the Lord comes, we will be in glory. We belong to a different day, a different dispensation, day of grace. Paul specifically included himself and other believers in the rapture by using the pronoun "we" (1 Thess. 4:15, 17), but notice that he excluded himself and his readers from the group who will see the coming day of the Lord.[1] Why should a child of God's grace—who is saved by grace, who is kept by grace, who has all the wonderful promises of God— be forced to go through a period which according to Scripture is expressly designed as a time of fearsome judgment on a Christ-rejecting world? We belong to the day; they belong to the night.

APPLYING THE TRUTH (5:6–11)

5:6–11 So then let us not sleep, as others do, but let us keep awake and be sober. For those who sleep, sleep at night, and those who get drunk, are drunk at night. But since we belong to the day, let us be sober, having put on the breastplate of faith and love, and for a helmet the hope of salvation. For God has not destined us for wrath, but to obtain salvation through our Lord Jesus Christ, who died for us so that whether we are awake or asleep we might live with him. Therefore encourage one another and build one another up, just as you are doing.

Verses 1–5 reveal that the day of the Lord will come suddenly, unannounced, and inescapably on an unbelieving world. But we as Christians will have no part in it because we do not belong to that period of time. In verses 6–11 Paul made the application of this glorious truth. All true prophetic teaching has an application. The study of prophecy is not just for prophecy's sake. God has taught us concerning future things because He wants us to be informed and, being informed, to be better Christians. One of the reasons for presenting the doctrine of Christ's imminent return is that it is an impelling motive to be living for Him every day. There is no better reason for working for Christ, apart from real love for Him, than the motive that we may see Him today. It makes a tremendous difference whether Christ is coming now, or whether we believe we will go through the tribulation and our only hope of seeing Him without dying is to survive that awful time of trouble. The imminency of the Lord's return is a precious, practical truth.

The hope of Christ's imminent return leads to this exhortation: "So then let us not sleep, as others do, but let us keep awake and be sober." The word *sober* in Greek means exactly what it means in English. It is the word for not being intoxicated. We are so prone to be intoxicated, not necessarily by alcohol but by the stimulants of the world—its glamour, pleasures, and appearance. Paul's message to these Christians reveals that we should be watching for the Lord's coming. If we realize the solemnity of the event for us and for those who will be left behind, how earnestly it should move us to watch and be sober! How we should be diligent in our Christian life and profession because of the imminent coming of Christ!

Paul went on: "But since we belong to the day, let us be sober, having put on the breastplate of faith and love, and for a helmet the hope of salvation" (v. 8). In 1 Thessalonians 1:3 Paul mentioned these same three entities—faith, love, and hope (cf. 1 Cor. 13:13). Because we belong to "the day," we are to go on in faith for the Lord. We are to put on the breastplate of faith and love, the best possible protection for spiritual battles. And the "helmet the hope of salvation" protects the mind. The sure hope of our final salvation is a great protection for our minds in dangerous, uncertain times when we are tempted to give in to discouragement and despair.

Verse 9 makes a wonderful declaration: "For God has not destined us for wrath, but to obtain salvation through our Lord Jesus Christ." Here Paul was saying expressly that our appointment is to be caught up to be with Christ; the appointment of the world is for the day of the Lord, the day of wrath. One cannot keep both of these appointments. We make our appointment for salvation and the rapture when we trust Jesus Christ as our Savior from sin. Certainly after the church is raptured, some in the tribulation will turn to Christ, and Revelation 7:9–10 states that there will be an innumerable company of martyrs. Many will be saved after the church has gone to heaven, but they will experience the awfulness of that period. As the wrath of God is poured upon the earth, it will involve them too.

Many believers who come to faith in Christ during the tribulation will also die during that terrible time. The reason they will be subjected to these things is that they were not ready for Christ when He came for His church. They had not trusted in Him at that time. But we who have trusted Him, who have believed in Christ as our Savior, are not appointed to that day of wrath. We are appointed to meet Christ in the air and to be forever with Him. This passage teaches that Christ is coming for His church *before* the day of the Lord begins, *before* the day of trouble—which is pictured in Revelation and all through the Bible—overtakes the world.

The basis for our hope in that day is that we will have obtained "salvation through our Lord Jesus Christ, who died for us so that whether we are awake or asleep we might live with him." In other words, whether we are "awake," that is, are alive at the time the Lord comes, or "asleep" and our bodies have been laid in the grave though our spirits have gone to heaven, when Christ comes back for His church there will be a wonderful reunion—both a rapture of the living saints and a resurrection of church-age believers from the dead. This is all based on our hope in the death of Christ.

Some who hold to the partial-rapture view think that only very spiritual Christians will be raptured before the tribulation, including of course those who hold this theory! They believe the less spiritual believers who are not ready will be taken up later in several subsequent raptures as they become ready. They interpret the words "asleep" and "awake" to refer to one's spiritual condition at the time of the Lord's coming, not to being alive or dead physically. Most of us would like to meet some of these especially spiritual folks who are good enough to be raptured with the first group. We may know many very fine Christians, but have we ever found one yet who was perfect? No, not yet.

If our being translated depended on our perfection, all of us would be required to go through the tribulation. Also, if the timing of our translation to heaven depends in some degree or other on our own spiritual maturity or readiness, how ready must we be? What degree of maturity or readiness is required to make it in the first group? The Bible never says. If, on the other hand, our being raptured depends on the death and the resurrection of Christ as this text indicates, then every true believer in Christ who has trusted in Him as his sacrifice for sin and as his Savior will be translated when Christ comes and will go home to glory with the Lord and with the loved ones who have gone on before. The only qualification for participation in the rapture, according to Scripture, is to be "in Christ" through faith in Him.

On the basis of this wonderful prospect, we should continue to "encourage" one another in the faith. As we look forward to the coming of the Lord, may it not only be a part of our theology and of our hope, but may it be the mainspring of our Christian life and testimony. If today is the last day on earth before Christ comes, may it be a day that is well spent in God's service for His glory and for the testimony of the truth!

NOTE

1. Thomas L. Constable, "1 Thessalonians," in *The Bible Knowledge Commentary*, New Testament, eds. John F. Walvoord and Roy B. Zuck (Wheaton, IL: Victor, 1983; repr., Colorado Springs: Cook, 1996), 705.

6 Living in Light of the Lord's Return
1 Thessalonians 5:12–28

While 1 Thessalonians unfolds many great doctrines, it closes with a very practical note. First, the general theme of our Christian testimony and relationships is presented. What do others see in our life? Our life and testimony are challenged in three key areas: our testimony toward our Christian leaders, our testimony toward one another, and our testimony toward the Lord.

TESTIMONY TOWARD CHRISTIAN LEADERS (5:12–13)

5:12–13 We ask you, brothers, to respect those who labor among you and are over you in the Lord and admonish you, and to esteem them very highly in love because of their work. Be at peace among yourselves.

Paul's exhortation to the Thessalonians to honor their spiritual leaders was rather unusual because of the circumstances in this church. That is, the church in Thessalonica had only been in existence for several months, so basically every member of this church was a new convert, although some were no doubt Jewish believers who knew the Old Testament Scriptures well. Some of them had probably been saved on the same day, or in the same week.

Still, God had called out from among the Thessalonians a few men to be their leaders. They had not had any training in a seminary, college, or Bible institute. All they had was what Paul had given them in his few short weeks in the city (cf. Acts 17:1–9), and what the Holy Spirit had taught them in the days and weeks that followed. But God had put His hand on some to be teachers and leaders, and some as elders or overseers of God's people. Thus

Paul's message to the church was, "Give recognition, esteem, and respect to those who have the gift of leadership."

It is naturally difficult for two Christians who start out the same way and have come from the same background to recognize that one is better than the other as far as administering the Lord's work is concerned. Some may have said of a leader, "Who is he to take the place of leadership in the church?" Paul was telling them to recognize people according to their ministry—not for what they were, but for what they were doing as ministers of the Lord. And these leaders were clearly working hard in their calling; the Greek verb translated "labor" in verse 12 can also mean to "work hard" or even "grow weary or tired." Thus Paul's instruction was for these hardworking leaders to be respected.

Christians are all alike in the sense that both the clergy and laity, the pastors and the people, are on the same level. But the Bible also teaches that we do not all have the same gifts. Some can teach; some can administer; some can help; some can evangelize. There is a difference in the opportunity and the way in which we serve the Lord. If a believer has gifts of teaching and of being a leader, other members in the church should recognize that and respond to these gifts and the exercise of them that God has given. The Thessalonians were exhorted to do this, and to accept the admonition given to them by those who teach.

In verse 13 Paul added, "Esteem them very highly in love because of their work." How carefully the apostle expressed it! He did not say: "Accept your leaders because they are unusually fine looking or well dressed, or because they have such fine gifts of oratory, or because they have personality and charisma." No doubt he could have commended those leaders about many things, but that was not the point. They should be esteemed because of the work they were doing. In other words, when we recognize that God is using someone, it is a recognition of God and His sovereign choice, of divine grace and gifts, and not of the person himself. The glory must remain with God even though we recognize the instrument. We are to esteem our leaders highly because of their work. While God expects us to be discerning and not to accept what is contrary to His Word, any criticism should be given in love and for the furtherance of God's work. We are clearly taught that we should esteem God's servants, even the humble ones, very highly for their work's sake.

Paul continued with the exhortation, "Be at peace among yourselves." There is a direct relationship between recognizing leadership and maintaining peace in the church. It is impossible for any work of God to be run by everyone. There must be someone who is responsible for different parts. It is possible to have too many cooks in the kitchen. That is also true in the work of the Lord. We can have too many people trying to run the church, demanding their own way. We should recognize leaders and pray for them, at the same time being willing to follow their leadership. Hebrews 13:17 reminds us, "Obey your leaders and submit to them, for they are keeping watch over your souls, as those who will have to give an account. Let them do this with joy and not with groaning, for that would be of no advantage to you." Allowing leaders to serve with joy helps secure peace and unity in the church. Of course, this does not mean we can never disagree with the leaders or express our legitimate concerns, but we must do all we can to maintain peace and submit to their leadership unless issues of essential doctrine are at stake. Peace among ourselves requires also that each person do his own work and not the work of someone else, responding to the plan and program as God has led in it.

TESTIMONY TOWARD OTHER CHRISTIANS (5:14–15)

5:14–15 And we urge you, brothers, admonish the idle, encourage the fainthearted, help the weak, be patient with them all. See that no one repays anyone evil for evil, but always seek to do good to one another and to everyone.

In these verses Paul addressed the believers' testimony and relationship toward their fellow Christians. The word *admonish* is the same Greek word translated "admonish" in verse 12. This word suggests the idea of "putting in mind" or "setting in mind." It means to warn in a sense of instructing or encouraging someone to do what is right. The "idle" in Thessalonica were lazy people who were neglecting their daily tasks. This same word is used in 2 Thessalonians 3:6, 7, 11. We are to admonish those who are not cooperating in the Lord's work, who are disorderly and out of step with the direction everyone else is headed. Apparently they had trouble even in that day with people who did not get in line and do the things they ought to do.

Then Paul told his readers to "encourage the fainthearted," or, better translated, "comfort the feeble in spirit" or "the weak-spirited." Literally the word means those who are "small souled." Some people are easily worried, fearful, and discouraged. We all know those who struggle under the weight of life's problems and get discouraged, afraid, and despondent more easily than others. All of us have had the experience of being very discouraged at times, and when someone spoke an encouraging word it helped us greatly. In this case the ministry of encouragement can be like a car with battery cables that comes alongside another car with a dead battery to give it a jump start, a transfer of power. The Lord wants us to come alongside those who are discouraged and give them a spiritual jump start.

We are also to support and "help the weak" (v. 14). The word here apparently refers to weakness in one's spiritual life. Some Christians are weak, that is, easily led astray. They have not learned to lean on Christ to support, help, and encourage them. This church of young Christians was exhorted to help the weak. The Greek word *antecheste*, translated "help," means "to hold yourself over against, to hold on to, cling to, hold up." The stronger sheep are to hold up the weaker ones.

At the same time they were commanded to "be patient with them all." While some require large doses of patience, every Christian needs to have a little patience administered to them at times. Do not expect anyone to be perfect, but have a little patience whenever it is required.

In verse 15 a great Christian principle is stated: "See that no one repays anyone evil for evil, but always seek to do good to one another and to everyone." Someone has said that there are three standards: first, the standard of the pagan world, which does evil in response to good; second, the standard of the so-called cultured world, which is to do good toward those who do good to them; third, the standard of Christian faith, which is to do good to those who do evil to us. This is contrary to the natural unsaved person; it is contrary to natural ethics, but it is according to the Word of God.

The Thessalonian Christians were told not to do wrong to people who had wronged them. Nor are they to take things into their own hands (Prov. 20:22; Matt. 5:38–39; Rom. 12:17, 19, 21). They were to refuse to retaliate. This was an absolute statement. There were no exceptions or loopholes. They were being persecuted for their faith and were having a hard time. How easy it would have been for them to "get even," as we say. But Paul said, "No, that is not the Christian way. The Christian way is to take evil and respond with good." Certainly that is what God has done for us. God has surely shown His love particularly for those who have trusted in Christ. God has taken the evil which resulted in the crucifixion of Christ, and in response to our sins God has given us grace and salvation. He has given us hope in the Lord Jesus.

TESTIMONY TOWARD GOD (5:16–23)

5:16–18 Rejoice always, pray without ceasing, give thanks in all circumstances; for this is the will of God in Christ Jesus for you.

In verses 16–23 the third aspect of our relationships in light of Christ's coming is presented, namely, our testimony toward God. The world can see only our outer life, but God knows what we are doing. He knows our heart, our attitude, and our spiritual life. Paul raised the ultimate question of all, "What does God think about us?" In answer to that question, the apostle gave the most simple and yet profound exhortation to be found anywhere in the Word.

Three exhortations are grouped together in verses 16–18. It is not as clear in the English as it is in the Greek New Testament. Verse 18 says, "for this is the will of God in Christ Jesus for you," and it seems clear from the Greek that these three commands—"rejoice," "pray," and "give thanks"—are summed up as a unit, as combining the will of God. We often wonder about God's will for our lives. It is one of the most asked questions by Christians: What is God's will for my life? Yet, here are three basic components of God's will for every Christian. Here is Christian testimony in relation to God in a very concise statement.

"Rejoice always" (v. 16) is the shortest verse in the Greek New Testament (John 11:35, "Jesus wept," is the shortest verse in the English Bible, but it is three words in Greek as opposed to two words here, and the three words of John 11:35 are longer than the two words of this verse). Even though verse 16 is the shortest verse in the Bible, it certainly says a great deal. One of the amazing things about the Word of God is that it can say so much in a few words.

Suppose that all that we knew about a Christian was that he or she rejoiced always. How much would we know? First, we could be sure that this person was genuinely saved. In ancient times the flying of the flag over a castle indicated that the king was in residence. It was taken down when he was gone. Someone has said that true joy can be described as "the flag that flies high above my heart to show that the King is in residence there." The world may have its pleasure, but it knows nothing of rejoicing always. For the Christian who is living in the will of God, there is the possibility of rejoicing always.

Second, rejoicing always also shows that a person is living in the realm of faith, trusting the Lord. Does that characterize our lives as God knows us? Consider the simple sin of murmuring and complaining as recorded in the book of Exodus and other books that tell of Israel's journey from Egypt to the Promised Land. God punished them severely for their murmuring. They complained about the same things we are apt to complain about: our food, our drink, our circumstances. But here in 1 Thessalonians 5:16 we have the opposite of murmuring.

Next Paul wrote, "Pray without ceasing." What does that mean? Does it mean we are to stay on our knees twenty-four hours a day? No, our Lord did not do that, and Paul did not either. It means, first of all, that Paul maintained his stated times of prayer. Daniel prayed three times a day. When the decree was given that he should not do it, what did he do? Did he stop? Did he cut out one of them? Or did he close the windows? No, he went right on, faithfully praying three times a day (Dan. 6:10). He continued in prayer without ceasing, praying at his stated times.

Second, we are to continue to pray at frequent intervals throughout the day. The same word translated here "without ceasing" (*adialeiptos*) is found earlier in 1 Thessalonians 1:2 ("constantly") and 2:13 ("constantly"). This word was used in ancient times of someone with a hacking cough. We all know what that is like. This does not mean that a person coughs continuously without stopping, but that he continually coughs off and on all through the day and night. That is a graphic picture of what it means to pray without ceasing. We are always to be in touch with God. Certainly two friends can be in the same room and be in harmony and fellowship with each other, even though they may not be talking with each other all the time. Paul is saying, "Do you want a rich experience? Begin a walk of fellowship with the Lord, not only at stated times of prayer, in which you bring all your needs to Him, but also the unbroken walk of communion—praying without ceasing."

The third command is, "Give thanks in all circumstances." Put these three things together, and you have a simple recipe for a happy Christian life. Giving thanks no matter the circumstance does not necessarily mean giving thanks *for* everything, although that statement is found in Ephesians 5:20, "giving thanks always and for everything to God the Father in the name of our Lord Jesus Christ." Giving thanks in all things or in every circumstance means that in every circumstance of life, no matter where God puts you, no matter what your difficulties, you can thank God for all He has done for you. You may be praying earnestly that He will change your circumstances. You may be praying for victory. You can thank God that in it all you will be victorious in Christ. So in everything give thanks. This is also God's will, as stated so plainly at the end of verse 18: "for this is the will of God in Christ Jesus for you." This is the second clear statement of God's will for every Christian in 1 Thessalonians (see also 4:3).

5:19–22 Do not quench the Spirit. Do not despise prophecies, but test everything; hold fast what is good. Abstain from every form of evil.

These four verses relate to the first command of this section, "Do not quench the Spirit." Paul had taught these new believers extensively about the

Holy Spirit (1:5, 6; 4:8). He had given them a crash course in *pneumatology*, the doctrine of the Holy Spirit. This tremendous doctrine in a word is this: When Christ went to heaven He sent the Holy Spirit. On the day of Pentecost every true believer in Christ was indwelt by the Spirit. Ever since, whenever a person trusts in Christ as his Savior, the Holy Spirit baptizes him into the body of Christ (1 Cor. 12:13), comes into his mortal body, and makes it a holy sanctuary, a temple of God (1 Cor. 6:19). The Holy Spirit is there to teach us, to guide us, to direct us, to convict us, to show us the way to understand the Scriptures, to give us joy and peace and love, and to transform our lives and our character and our experience.

The ministries of the Holy Spirit are both manifold and magnificent! Yet, we have within us the capacity to quench or stifle the Spirit. This means to put out or extinguish His fire in our lives. Sometimes we see Christians who we know are saved, but their lives do not reflect the fragrance of the presence of God. What is wrong with them? They are resisting the Holy Spirit. What does it mean to quench the Spirit? It means saying "no" to God, "no" to something to which the Spirit is saying "yes." We should instead always be saying, "Yes, Lord."

In yielding to the Lord and His will, the Thessalonian Christians were told they should, first, not despise prophecies. Further, they were to "test everything." To "test" means to examine, sift, and weigh. In other words, not everything they heard was necessarily prophesied. It was not necessarily from God. They had to distinguish between truth and error, even as we do today as we listen to others preach and teach God's Word. We must not believe everything we hear without testing and sifting it first. We must hold to what is good and put away what is bad. In verse 22 Paul summed up what it means to not quench the Spirit, "Abstain from every form of evil." The word "abstain" means to hold yourself off from. We have the broad statement that regardless of what it is in our lives that may be contrary to the will of God, whether counterfeit teaching or sinful living, it should be taken out of our lives.

5:23 Now may the God of peace himself sanctify you completely, and may your whole spirit and soul and body be kept blameless at the coming of our Lord Jesus Christ.

Here Paul contemplated the time when we will be perfect and blameless in the presence of God. God has indeed set us apart to holy living. This does not mean that we are perfect now. But it does mean that we should be holy, set apart in life and thinking to the Lord and His purposes. The word *whole* here refers to our spirit, our soul, and our body. Each of these three parts should be preserved holy to God and be used by God. That means that everything we are belongs to Him—our physical bodies, our spiritual or intellectual life, and our psychological or natural life.

CONCLUDING EXHORTATIONS (5:24–28)

5:24–28 He who calls you is faithful; he will surely do it. Brothers, pray for us. Greet all the brothers with a holy kiss. I put you under oath before the Lord to have this letter read to all the brothers. The grace of our Lord Jesus Christ be with you.

No one can sanctify himself. God has to set us apart as holy to Himself, and the great truth here is that He will be faithful to do it. God will bring it to pass.

Verse 25 is a very understandable exhortation: "Brothers, pray for us." We need prayer. It takes prayer and the work of the Holy Spirit to accomplish any significant work for God. In 2 Thessalonians 3:1 Paul again asked these believers to pray for him and his companions.

He then closed with a greeting in 1 Thessalonians 5:26 to all the believers that included "a holy kiss." This is commanded four other times in the New Testament (Rom. 16:16; 1 Cor. 16:20; 2 Cor. 13:12; 1 Pet. 5:14). A hug and a kiss on the cheek, men with men and women with women, were the cultural expression of greeting and of their oneness in God's family. The word *holy* "underlines that it is not to be an expression of romantic love but of distinctly Christian love toward fellow believers. It is the sign of a sanctified spiritual relationship."[1]

In verse 27 we read, "I put you under oath before the Lord to have this letter read to all the brothers." This is the fifth time in verses 12–27 that Paul used the word "brothers," which encompassed both men and women (vv. 12, 14, 25, 26, 27). This reveals that the church is a family. Paul charged them to have the epistle read. He was conscious of the fact that this was the very Word of God. Paul then closed this letter with that great benediction: "The grace of our Lord Jesus Christ be with you." As Paul wrote this to the Thessalonian Christians, so may the grace of God, His favor, His enablement, be made real in all our lives.

NOTE

1. D. Edmond Hiebert, *1 and 2 Thessalonians* (Chicago: Moody, 1971), 276.

7

A Pastoral Word of Comfort
2 Thessalonians 1:1–12

SALUTATION (1:1–2)

1:1–2 Paul, Silvanus, and Timothy, to the church of the Thessalonians in God our Father and the Lord Jesus Christ: Grace to you and peace from God our Father and the Lord Jesus Christ.

Second Thessalonians opens with a salutation that is practically word for word the same as the first epistle. Silas, called Silvanus here, and Timothy joined Paul in this letter as well as in 1 Thessalonians. Paul and Silas had brought the gospel to the Thessalonians and Timothy had visited them to bring encouragement, and so together they sent their greetings.

The mention of "the church of the Thessalonians" reminds us again that the church is people. Also, again they are said to be "in God our Father and the Lord Jesus Christ" (v. 1). Though their earthly circumstance was one of great trial and affliction, their position before God, like that of all other believers, was secure in Christ and in the Father. No other religion says this. People are never said to be "in Buddha" or "in Confucius" or "in Allah or Muhammad." Yet, believers are in vital union with Christ. It is a marvelous truth that we as Christians have the same position in Christ regardless of circumstances, whether we face trials or joy. The fact that we are in Christ continues unchanged all through our lives and then throughout eternity.

Verse 2 is Paul's trademark apostolic greeting. It would be difficult to find two words in Scripture more meaningful than "grace" and "peace." They represent God's answer to the greatest need of the human heart. Grace, a relationship between God and individuals, is established and based on the fact that Christ died for sinners, resulting in God's unmerited favor—God giving to sinful people the opposite of what they deserve. Grace gives eternal life, blessing, and promises for joy throughout eternity instead of judgment, which all of us justly deserve.

Coupled with grace is peace. How the human heart longs for peace. Much is involved in this word. All Christians have peace *with* God through faith in Christ (Rom. 5:1). The enmity or the wrath of God has been put aside, and we are the objects of His favor. Also, Christians can have the peace *of* God, the *experience* of peace (Phil. 4:6). This is probably what is meant in this passage of Scripture. Paul wanted the Thessalonians not only to realize that everything was right between them and the Lord, but also that they might experience God's peace in their trials and afflictions. Paul was reminding his readers that, although they were enduring trouble and persecution, they were, nevertheless, the recipients of God's wonderful grace and His satisfying peace.

THANKSGIVING FOR THEIR
GROWING FAITH AND LOVE (1:3–5)

1:3–5 We ought always to give thanks to God for you, brothers, as is right, because your faith is growing abundantly, and the love of every one of you for one another is increasing. Therefore we ourselves boast about you in the churches of God for your steadfastness and faith in all your persecutions and in the afflictions that you are enduring. This is evidence of the righteous judgment of God, that you may be considered worthy of the kingdom of God, for which you are also suffering.

As in his first letter to the Thessalonians Paul bore testimony a second time to their faithfulness to God in all their troubles. When this good news arrived from Timothy, Paul gave thanks for these believers. The word "ought" (sometimes translated "bound") is the word for paying a debt. Paul was saying that he owed it to them to thank God always for them. Certainly thanksgiving is fitting. Sometimes Christians forget to thank God for things He has done for them.

Two things in particular occasioned Paul's thanksgiving—their faith and their love, both of which were growing. The Thessalonian Christians had come to know Christ as their Savior only a few months before. But from that moment on, they believed in God and in Christ. But Paul was not talking about the fact of their faith, but that their faith was "growing abundantly." It was enlarging. Few things are more exciting than seeing people growing in their faith.

How is it possible for one's faith to grow? Is not faith in Christ as Savior enough? Yes, it is enough for salvation, but there is still room for deeper experience. While a Christian will not question the deity of Christ and the sufficiency of His wonderful salvation provided through His death and resurrection, a believer can learn by experience to trust the Lord concerning *all* things. That is a process of spiritual education. As Christians go through life, they learn to trust God. They find by experience that He is altogether trustworthy and that they can trust Him not only regarding their eternal future, but also regarding matters in this life. In other words, it is possible to grow in faith as one's trust in God increases and expands.

Some Christians are perfectly willing to trust God about eternity, but their problems of today and tomorrow seem to them too big and overwhelming to commit to the Lord. Of course, it is unreasonable and ridiculous to trust God about eternal things and not trust Him about temporal things, but that is human nature. The Thessalonians, however, were in a position where they had to trust God daily. They were in constant danger of losing their very lives. In this situation their faith grew, and that is what trials are designed to do for us. Tribulation works patience, patience experience, and experience hope (cf. Rom. 5:3–4). A good question for each of us to ask is, "How is my faith? Is it growing? Do I trust the Lord more now than when I first believed?"

Paul also commended these believers for their love, which was "increasing." Trusting the Lord is one thing, but having a true love for our brothers and sisters in Christ is another. Sometimes in our churches there is little evidence of heresy, but there is also little evidence of love for the brethren. The Scriptures bear witness that in the Thessalonian church the believers not only increased in faith, but they also loved each other and that love expanded. In many ways this Thessalonian church was an ideal, model Christian assembly.

Therefore Paul was able to "boast about you [the Thessalonians] in the churches of God" because of their faithfulness in persecution and their growing faith and love. He used this church as an illustration. The word for "steadfastness" is a very significant word in the Greek New Testament. It means to "remain under." Christians have burdens and cares, which they would like to get rid of. Sometimes they become frustrated and impatient with a situation. But the person who is patient "remains under" and keeps carrying the load that is given him, and adjusts himself to his circumstances. He regards his situation as something that God has given him. These Thessalonian Christians are described as having a testimony that grew, a love that increased and abounded, and a steadfastness that continued. These three words hark back to 1 Thessalonians 1:3. The church was strong in faith, love, and steadfastness. This certainly is a marvelous testimony and example for believers today to emulate.

Paul then contrasted the believers' situation to that of their persecutors (v. 5). Here is a profound principle, though it is not stated explicitly in this verse. For the Christian the present age is a day of suffering, trial, and temptation, but in the future the glory will be ours. This is the pattern Christ Himself experienced—suffering first and then glory, the cross and then the crown.

The pattern for the world is just the opposite. The ideal for the world is to eat, drink, and be merry now, for suffering will follow. Judgment will come later. This world is the best it will ever be for an unbeliever and the worst it will ever be for a believer. As the old saying goes, "This world is the only heaven the lost will ever know and the only hell the believer will ever experience." The Thessalonians were undergoing severe trials, but this was compelling evidence to them of their future glory. The very fact that they were experiencing trials caused by their persecutors was a sign that the latter would be tried and judged in the future. The result for these Christians was that they would be counted worthy of the kingdom of God for which they were suffering.

THE COMING JUDGMENT
OF GOD ON THE UNSAVED (1:6–12)

1:6–9 Since indeed God considers it just to repay with affliction those who afflict you, and to grant relief to you who are afflicted as well as to us, when the Lord Jesus is revealed from heaven with his mighty angels in flaming fire, inflicting vengeance on those who do not know God and on those who do not obey the gospel of our Lord Jesus. They will suffer the punishment of eternal destruction, away from the presence of the Lord and from the glory of his might.

In verses 6–9 the judgment on the unsaved is grippingly portrayed as occurring at the second coming of Christ. That Jesus is coming again accompanied by angels is the consistent witness of Scripture (Zech. 14:5; Matt. 13:39–42; 25:31).

This portion of Scripture is very clear that the destiny of the evil is something horrible to contemplate. The judgment of the living unsaved will take place at the time Christ returns to earth with His holy angels. The character of that judgment is plainly depicted. It is a judgment of "flaming fire, inflicting vengeance on those who do not know God and on those who do not obey the gospel of our Lord Jesus. They will suffer the punishment of eternal destruction, away from the presence of the Lord and from the glory of his might." Some teach that "eternal destruction" refers to the annihilation of the lost, but the word "destruction" could be translated "ruination." They will not be destroyed in the sense of extinction or ceasing to exist, but will experience eternal ruin. The Bible teaches that the lost will continue to exist forever in the lake of fire (Matt. 25:46; Mark 9:43, 48; Rev. 14:10–11).

The recipients of God's judgment are described as "those who do not know God and . . . who do not obey the gospel." These may refer to one group, with the second phrase being a further explanation or definition of the first. However, it is better to view these as referring to two groups that will experience God's judgment: "those who do not know God" are pagans without the full knowledge of God and the gospel, while "those who do not obey the gospel of our Lord Jesus" are those who have clearly heard the truth and willfully rejected it. Hiebert supports this view and says, "The second class is more guilty than the first. The first class is guilty of ignorance of God, but it is a reprehensible ignorance, resulting from their rejection of the light they did have (Rom. 1:18–23). The second class is identified by its refusal to obey, to listen and submit to, the gospel. . . . They not only reject the knowledge offered in the gospel but also refuse the obedience the gospel demands."[1]

True, the Thessalonian believers were going through trials, but the prospect before them was one of glory, reward, and eternal blessing. The prospect before their persecutors was one of terrible judgment from God, as is pictured here. Once again the contrast is drawn between trial and trouble as it comes to the Christian, and the just judgment of God that will overtake those who do not know Him and those who refuse to obey and believe the gospel.

THE COMING OF THE LORD (1:10)

1:10 when he comes on that day to be glorified in his saints, and to be marveled at among all who have believed, because our testimony to you was believed.

The time of this terrifying judgment will occur when Christ returns to be glorified in His people and to set up His earthly kingdom. In the Scriptures in general, and in 1–2 Thessalonians particularly, a contrast is drawn between the coming of Christ for His church, which is pictured in 1 Thessalonians 4:13–18, and His coming to earth to set up His millennial, messianic kingdom. At His coming for His church, the dead in Christ will rise first and living Christians will be caught up to be with the Lord. John 14:1–3 reveals that after the church is raptured, Christ will take her to heaven to be with the Father in the Father's house in the place Christ has prepared. This is the glorious prospect for the Thessalonians as well as for us who have trusted in Christ.

In the Thessalonian epistles the Lord's coming to the earth to set up His kingdom is also revealed. This event is not the same as His coming for His church. The following chart highlights the differences between these two future phases of the Lord's coming.

THE RAPTURE	THE RETURN (Second Coming)
Christ comes in the air (1 Thess. 4:16–17)	Christ comes to the earth (Zech. 14:4)
Christ comes for His saints (1 Thess. 4:16–17)	Christ comes with His saints (1 Thess. 3:13; Jude 14)
Believers depart the earth (1 Thess. 4:16–17)	Unbelievers are taken away (Matt. 24:37–41)
Christ claims His bride (Matt. 25:1–13)	Christ comes with His bride (Rev. 19:7)
Christ gathers His own (1 Thess. 4:16–17)	Angels gather the elect (Matt. 24:31)
Christ comes to reward (1 Thess. 4:17)	Christ comes to judge (Matt. 25:31–46)
Not in the Old Testament (1 Cor. 15:51)	Predicted often in the Old Testament (Dan. 7:13–14, etc.)
There are no signs; it is imminent (1 Thess. 5:1–3)	Portended by many signs (Matt. 24:4–29)
It is a time of blessing and comfort (1 Thess. 4:18)	It is a time of destruction and judgment (2 Thess. 2:8–12)
Involves believers only (John 14:1–3; 1 Cor. 15:51–55; 1 Thess. 4:13–18)	Involves Israel and the Gentile nations (Matt. 24:1–25:46)
Will occur in a moment, in the time it takes to blink. Only His own will see Him (1 Cor. 15:51–52)	Will be visible to the entire world (Matt. 24:27; Rev. 1:7)
Tribulation begins (Rev. 6)	Millennium begins (Rev. 20)
Christ comes as the bright morning star (Rev. 22:16)	Christ comes as the sun of righteousness (Mal. 4:2)

The question arises in 2 Thessalonians 1:10 as to which phase of His coming is being discussed. The best explanation seems to be that in this verse Christ is referring to the coming to establish His kingdom. When He comes to take His church home to glory, the earth is not judged. The church will be taken out of the world very quickly—in a moment, in the twinkling of an eye—and will be taken to heaven. Christ also goes back with the church to heaven. His purpose will not be to judge the evil then.

When Christ comes back to establish His kingdom, however, the Scriptures make it clear that He will judge the world in perfect righteousness. This judgment is illustrated in Matthew 25. He will gather the Gentiles before Him and separate the sheep from the goats, that is, separate the saved from the lost:

When the Son of Man comes in his glory, and all the angels with him, then he will sit on his glorious throne. Before him will be gathered all the nations, and he will separate people one from another as a shepherd separates the sheep from the goats. And he will place the sheep on his right, but the goats on the left. (Matt. 25:31–33)

This judgment has to do with the living people in the world at the time of His second coming. Ezekiel 20 reveals that Christ will judge the Jews in a similar manner when He regathers them from all over the world and purges out the rebels from among them:

I will bring you out from the peoples and gather you out of the countries where you are scattered, with a mighty hand and an outstretched arm, and with wrath poured out. And I will bring you into the wilderness of the peoples, and there I will enter into judgment with you face to face. As I entered into judgment with your fathers in the wilderness of the land of Egypt, so I will enter into judgment with you, declares the Lord God. I will make you pass under the rod, and I will bring you into the bond of the covenant. I will purge out the rebels from among you, and those who transgress against me. I will bring them out of the land where they sojourn, but they shall not enter the land of Israel. Then you will know that I am the LORD. (Ezek. 20:34–38)

In other words, when Christ comes back it will be a time of separation of the wheat from the tares (Matt. 13:24–30). He will separate the saved from the lost.

The very fact that Christ is coming back in such power and glory will result in many marveling at His power and glory. When He comes back He will be accompanied by the saints. The event will be such a tremendous spectacle that it will impel worship and admiration on the part of all who believe, as described in verse 10. This will be true not only of the church, which is with Christ as His bride, but it will be true of all others who will be included in the term *saints*, including Old Testament and tribulation believers.

THE NEED FOR PRAYER (1:11–12)

1:11–12 To this end we always pray for you, that our God may make you worthy of his calling and may fulfill every resolve for good and every work of faith by his power, so that the name of our Lord Jesus may be glorified in you, and you in him, according to the grace of our God and the Lord Jesus Christ.

In verse 11 Paul applied the truth to his own prayer life. God did not reveal future things simply to satisfy our curiosity, but for the purpose of presenting practical truth on which we should base our lives. This was the point Paul made here. He reviewed the Thessalonians' sufferings, and how God was able to take care of them. He discussed how evil would be punished in due time. Then he made the application. Since this is our destiny, since glory is ahead, and since we will be in the very presence of our glorious Savior, what an exhortation to live for Christ right now! Paul prayed constantly that this truth would be fulfilled in his readers' lives.

Paul must have had a long prayer list and must have spent a great deal of time in prayer. The burden of this prayer was that God would count them worthy of this calling. He did not mean by this that they were worthy of salvation, because no one could ever be worthy. No one can merit God's mercy and forgiveness. Instead Paul meant that since believers in Christ have such a glorious destiny, they should lead lives that are in keeping with this truth. In this sense they would be "worthy of his calling and . . . fulfill every resolve for good and every work of faith by his power."

Glorifying the name of Christ was to be the ultimate goal of the Thessalonians' experience—whether by testimony, or by enduring tribulation. In other words, as they led their lives, sometimes in real affliction and trial, they could nevertheless live in such a way as to bring honor and glory to the Savior. As we experience various problems and face different opportunities for service, is it true of us, as it was of these believers so long ago, that our lives are the means of bringing glory to the Savior? Are we manifesting Christ as His trophies of grace, giving evidence that we belong to Him and He belongs to us?

What does it mean to bring glory to Christ? This expression is often used, but perhaps is not always analyzed or understood as it should be. We talk about "glorifying God," or we pray that a church service or some activity might "glorify the Lord." What does this mean in everyday life?

The Scriptures state, "The heavens declare the glory of God, and the sky above proclaims his handiwork. Day to day pours out speech, and night to night reveals knowledge" (Ps. 19:1–2). What does it mean that the heavens declare the glory of God? The heavens manifest His wisdom, His power, and His purpose in designing all creation for an intelligent end. The heavens reveal what God is and what He can do. But the heavens are not designed to reveal the love, the grace, or the righteousness of God. That is where Christians come into the picture. We are designed to "show the immeasurable riches of his grace in kindness toward us in Christ Jesus" (Eph. 2:7).

To manifest the glory of God, we must become a living illustration, an incarnation, of what the power and the grace of God can do. Therefore as we yield our lives to the Lord and seek to serve Him, and put Him on display and make Him known, we are able to glorify God. In other words, our daily life and testimony can be an example of what God's grace can do for us. The result is that "the name of our Lord Jesus Christ [is] glorified" in us.

An additional thought is given in verse 12: Christians are also glorified "in Christ." This is more than simply the matter of our glorifying God. Not only can Christ be glorified in us, but also we can be glorified in Him. But what does this mean? We are positioned in Christ because we have trusted in Him. When He is glorified, we are glorified in Him. This is His contribution to us and will be fulfilled particularly when He presents us in glory "according to the grace of our God and the Lord Jesus Christ."

In this first chapter some of the practical things that undergirded the Thessalonian church have been considered. Paul's thanksgiving for their faith in the midst of persecution was declared. In contrast to their temporary trouble, the coming eternal judgment of the unsaved was revealed. The chapter closed with their need for prayer, as Paul prayed that in their trials and afflictions they would truly manifest the glory of God in their faithfulness and testimony.

What was true for the church at Thessalonica is certainly the standard for us as well. As we face these Scriptures in this modern generation, God challenges us, regardless of our circumstances or difficulties, to lead a life that is faithful and well-pleasing in His sight, bringing honor and glory to His name as we look for His coming.

NOTE

1. D. Edmond Hiebert, *1 and 2 Thessalonians* (Chicago: Moody, 1971), 313.

The Revelation of the Man of Lawlessness
2 Thessalonians 2:1–12

In chapter 2, Paul moved from affirmation to explanation, from comfort in the face of persecution to caution in the face of false teaching, from a pastoral word to a prophetic word. Second Thessalonians 2 is one of the great prophetic chapters of Scripture. No other chapter in the entire Bible covers precisely the same points of revelation that are given here.

FALSE TEACHING IN THESSALONICA (2:1–3)

2:1–2 Now concerning the coming of our Lord Jesus Christ and our being gathered together to him, we ask you, brothers, not to be quickly shaken in mind or alarmed, either by a spirit or a spoken word, or a letter seeming to be from us, to the effect that the day of the Lord has come.

The occasion for this new revelation was the rise of false teaching in the Thessalonian church. The core of the false teaching was that they had already been plunged headlong into the day of the Lord, or tribulation. Their current persecution supported this false idea that they were in this predicted time of divine judgment, the tribulation, from which they had been promised deliverance in 1 Thessalonians 5:1–9.

If this was true, it would further mean either that Paul's previous teaching about their deliverance from that time was wrong, or that Paul had been correct and they had been left behind at the rapture. Neither of these prospects was appealing, and they were seriously shaken "with the impact of a major earthquake, and they were continuing to feel the disturbing aftershocks of that report."[1] In answer to this false teaching, Paul not only gave them assurance that they were not in this period, but he also gave them definite, discernible signs of the tribulation, which cannot occur while the church is still in the world.

The opening verses of the chapter get straight to the heart of the problem. The Thessalonians had been taught by someone that they were in the day of the Lord, that this fearful period of divine judgment had already overtaken them. This troubled and upset them because it was not what Paul had taught them earlier (cf. 1 Thess. 1:10; 4:13–5:9).

The false teaching had come to them by one of the three methods mentioned in verse 2: "by a spirit or a spoken word, or a letter seeming to be from us." Some had claimed that the Spirit of God had revealed this to them as a special revelation. Paul flatly contradicted this as a teaching of God. He also denied that he had sent any word orally to this effect. Further, he declared that he had not written this to them in a letter. Apparently they had received a forged, spurious letter that claimed to be from Paul, teaching that they were in the day of the Lord. But Paul said in effect, "I did not write such a letter." If such a letter had been written, it must have been a forgery. The teaching that the day of the Lord had fallen on the Thessalonians was therefore labeled as false doctrine, and their fears of being in this awful period were groundless.

In order to understand the nature of the error Paul is correcting, it is necessary to define what is meant by "the day of the Lord." This expression is found often in the Bible (nineteen times in the Old Testament and four times in the New Testament). In a word, it is the period of time predicted in the Scriptures when God will deal *directly* and *dramatically* in judgment or in blessing. It includes the tribulation time preceding the second advent of Christ, when He will deal with human sin directly, and it includes the millennial reign of Christ when He will directly pour out His blessings. It will culminate in the judgment of the great white throne (Rev. 20:11–15). The day of the Lord is therefore an extended period of time lasting over one thousand years that unfolds in two distinct phases—a seven-year judgment phase and a one-thousand-year blessing phase. This is brought out in the events included in the day of the Lord, presented in connection with the study of

1 Thessalonians 5:1–9. For more about the day of the Lord, see the section dealing with those verses.

Our present time, this current church age, is a day of grace. God is not attempting in our day to deal directly with human sin. He may impose judgment in some cases; but there are many evil people who flourish, who have health and wealth; they may succeed in business, even though they are not Christians and are not honoring the Lord. The Lord is not attempting to straighten that out in this day of grace. The overriding purpose of God in this age is to proclaim His grace, that people may be saved by trusting in Christ and receiving God's gift of grace.

In the day of the Lord, however, God will deal directly and dramatically with human sin. The Scriptures clearly present the fact that the day of the Lord is a day of divine judgment on the world. In the day of the Lord, Christ will rule with a rod of iron over the entire earth (Ps. 2:9; Rev. 2:27). He will administer absolute justice (Isa. 11:1–9). In that day Israel will be regathered (Isa. 11:10–12) and brought into the blessed peace of the millennial kingdom (Zeph. 3:14–20). In a word, there is a time of divine judgment coming, the day of the Lord, in which God will deal directly with this evil world.

2:3 Let no one deceive you in any way. For that day will not come, unless the rebellion comes first, and the man of lawlessness is revealed, the son of destruction.

The question that faced the Thessalonians, however, was whether their present sufferings were evidence that they were in this predicted period. Paul answered this question in effect, "No, you will not enter that period. The Lord will come for you first." To make this doctrine clear, some of the things that occur at the beginning of the day of the Lord were revealed. Because these events had not taken place, it demonstrated that the day of the Lord had not yet begun. The Thessalonians could not be in this period because certain things had to happen first. So Paul urged them not to be deceived.

Verse 3 states that two things must occur before the day of the Lord and the time of judgment can begin. The first is "the rebellion." This word is literally "the apostasy," which means a falling away or a departure. The meaning is the same here, to depart from in a doctrinal sense. In fact, our English word *apostasy* comes from the very Greek word used here (*apostasia*).

Paul was telling the Thessalonians, then, that this day of the Lord cannot come until there is a widespread departure from the true faith in God. Some have understood the term "the apostasy" to be the physical departure of the church itself—that is, the rapture, since the rapture will be a physical departure of believers from the earth. If this view were correct it would definitely place the rapture before the tribulation—a clear defense of the pretribulational rapture position. While this view is attractive to pretribulationists to support our view, there are six main reasons to reject this meaning of *apostasia* in this context:

1. In classical Greek *hē apostasia* ("the apostasy") was used to denote a political or military rebellion.
2. In the Septuagint (the Greek translation of the Old Testament) *hē apostasia* was used of rebellion against God (Josh. 22:22; Jer. 2:19).
3. In 2 Maccabees 2:15 (a noncanonical book written in the time between the Old and New Testaments) the word is used of apostasy to paganism.
4. In Acts 21:21, the only other use of the noun in the New Testament, apostasy refers to spiritual departure from Moses.
5. The rapture is not an act of departure by the saints; the saints are passive, not active.
6. In 2 Thessalonians 2:1 Paul referred to the rapture as "our gathering together to him." It seems strange to use this unlikely term ("the apostasy") for the same thing in the immediate context.[2]

For these reasons, most expositors have understood "the rebellion" (apostasy) in 2 Thessalonians 2:3 not as the physical departure of the church at the rapture, but rather as doctrinal departure from the truth. At the time 2 Thessalonians was written there were, no doubt, some errors in the church, but there was no widespread apostasy in the ordinary sense of the term. The churches were still true to the Lord. Paul was declaring that the day of the Lord cannot come until there is first a pervasive, global departure from the faith.

The Scriptures speak often of this coming apostasy. "Now the Spirit expressly says that in later times some will depart from the faith by devoting themselves to deceitful spirits and teachings of demons, through the insincerity of liars whose consciences are seared, who forbid marriage and require abstinence from foods that God created to be received with thanksgiving by those who believe and know the truth" (1 Tim. 4:1–3). In 2 Timothy 3:1, 13, Paul wrote, "But understand this, that in the last days there will come times of difficulty. . . . [E]vil people and impostors will go on from bad to worse, deceiving and being deceived." Again, Paul wrote, "For the time is coming when people will not endure sound teaching, but having itching ears they will accumulate for themselves teachers to suit their own passions, and will turn away from listening to the truth and wander off into myths" (2 Tim. 4:3–4). The book of Jude, which portrays spiritual apostasy that has crept into the church, has been described as the "foyer" or "introduction" of the book of Revelation. The Scriptures, then, predict that before this time of judgment can come, there must come first a turning away from true faith in God on the part of the professing church.

The situation today is entirely different from what it was for the Thessalonian church. Today there is certainly widespread apostasy. The sad fact is that many are not preaching the true gospel and, moreover, are denying the central doctrines of the Christian faith. Many are teaching that Christ is only a man, that He was not born of a virgin, that He was not sinless, that He did not rise from the dead, that salvation is not through His shed blood, and that He is not coming again. They deny that the Scriptures are the inerrant, infallible Word of God, and turn instead to some other forms of teaching. They reject the biblical standards for holy living and accept practices such as homosexuality, even among church leaders. To a certain degree, apostasy is already here and is surging in strength and intensity.

THE COMING OF THE MAN OF LAWLESSNESS (2:4–5)

2:4–5 who opposes and exalts himself against every so-called god or object of worship, so that he takes his seat in the temple of God, proclaiming himself to be God. Do you not remember that when I was still with you I told you these things?

The Scriptures indicate, however, that this present stage of turning away from the truth is just the beginning—just a faint foreshadow of the tsunami of error that is coming and will culminate in the day of the Lord. The apostasy that today is general, yet deepening, will swell and become more specific. It will be directed by the person mentioned here as the "man of lawlessness" or a man of sin—a man who is opposed to God. He is called "man of lawlessness" because this is his chief characteristic. Just as we refer to Christ as the "man of sorrows" because He endured much sorrow, so this person is a "man of lawlessness." His very life is characterized by blasphemous, arrogant sin and rebellion against God.

Verse 4 says this figure "takes his seat in the temple of God, proclaiming himself to be God." This means there will be a rebuilt, third Jewish temple standing on the temple mount in Jerusalem during the future day of the Lord (cf. Matt. 24:15; Rev. 11:1–2). The coming man of lawlessness will sit in this temple and desecrate it much as did the Syrian monarch Antiochus IV, known as Epiphanes, with the second temple in 167 B.C. Antiochus offered a pig, an unclean animal, on the altar of God in the temple, and placed an image of Zeus, that just happened to look like Antiochus, in the Most Holy Place. This appalling act of desecration will foreshadow the final abomination by this coming lawless one (Dan. 8:11–13; 9:27; 11:31; 12:11).

Most prophecy scholars and teachers believe that the "man of lawlessness" is a reference to the future world dictator, the same man described as the Antichrist in 1 John 2:18 and the beast out of the sea of Revelation 13:1. The final great apostasy is embodied and ultimately headed up in a man who has not yet appeared. The day of the Lord, therefore, could not have come in the Thessalonians' time because this evil person had not yet been revealed.

TEN TITLES OF THE FINAL WORLD DICTATOR

1. The little horn (Dan. 7:8)

2. A king, insolent and skilled in intrigue (Dan. 8:23)

3. The prince who is to come (Dan. 9:26)

4. The one who makes desolate (Dan. 9:27)

5. The king who does as he pleases (Dan. 11:36–45)

6. A foolish shepherd (Zech. 11:15–17)

7. The son of destruction (2 Thess. 2:3)

8. The lawless one (2 Thess. 2:8)

9. The rider on the white horse (Rev. 6:2)

10. The beast out of the sea (Rev. 13:1–2)

Swindoll describes the coming apostasy and Antichrist in this way:

This man is yet to be revealed and won't be until the dark age of apostasy engulfs the world. This man will emerge after the Rapture, probably to calm the chaotic waters troubled by the unexplained departure of so many Christians. He will be primed and ready to speak. He will stand before not only a nation but a world and will win their approval. Like Hitler, he will emerge on a scene of such political and economic chaos that the people will see him as a man with vision, with pragmatic answers and power to unite the world.[3]

In verse 5 Paul added this word: "Do you not remember that when I was still with you I told you these things?" One of the remarkable facts about the Thessalonian church was that Paul had taught them so much in so short a time, and that he was not hesitant to teach prophecy to young converts. When Paul came to Thessalonica, there was not a single Christian there.

When he left after only a few weeks of ministry, a small church had been formed. He had not only led them to Christ, but he had taught them a great deal of doctrine, including some of the deep things of the prophetic word. Now he reminds them of what he had taught them.

THE RESTRAINER OF EVIL (2:6–8)

2:6–8 And you know what is restraining him now so that he may be revealed in his time. For the mystery of lawlessness is already at work. Only he who now restrains it will do so until he is out of the way. And then the lawless one will be revealed, whom the Lord Jesus will kill with the breath of his mouth and bring to nothing by the appearance of his coming.

In verse 6, Paul gave another reason the Thessalonians were not in the day of the Lord: the presence of a restraining force that is preventing the man of lawlessness, the Antichrist (the "he" of v. 6), from being revealed. Here is the reason for the delay in the Antichrist entering the world spotlight—an obstacle that has to be removed before he can make his grand entry and the day of the Lord can begin. This tells us that God has a timetable for His program that Satan cannot change. As Wiersbe notes, "Just as there was a 'fullness of the time' for the coming of Christ (Gal. 4:4), so there is a 'fullness of the time' for the appearance of the Antichrist; and nothing will be off schedule."[4]

The "lawless one" in verse 8 is another reference to the Antichrist. He can be revealed only when what is restraining his manifestation is taken away. So the obvious question that needs to be answered is the identity of this one called "he who now restrains." In verse 6 the restrainer is described as an indefinite thing, a "what" (the terms are neuter), while verse 7 has the masculine pronoun "he." This clearly indicates that the restrainer is both an impersonal force or principle and a person. Expositors differ on what is meant. Even the best of Bible scholars who honor the Word of God do not necessarily agree on the identity of the restrainer. Many explanations have been offered.

One interpretation is that the man of sin was Nero, the Roman emperor. He was so evil that he was restrained by Seneca, a Roman statesman, until Nero contrived to have Seneca put out of the way. Then Nero was released and could do as he pleased. He burned many Christians at the stake and brought much persecution on the church. But this explanation is not correct. The events predicted to follow the day of the Lord, such as the second coming of Christ, did not occur after Nero's time. The man of sin could not have been Nero and the restrainer could not have been Seneca.

One honored scholar says the restrainer of evil is Satan. This teacher's idea is that Satan is holding back evil in its true character and that restraint will be removed in the time of the tribulation and then sin will be revealed in its true picture. Some truth may be in the fact that Satan does not always manifest sin in its real nature, for sometimes he "disguises himself as an angel of light" (2 Cor. 11:14). But certainly the Bible does not teach that Satan actually restrains sin. The Bible from Genesis to Revelation teaches exactly the opposite. Satan is revealed as doing and promoting all the evil he can. Furthermore, Satan is not taken away during the tribulation when evil reaches its peak. This interpretation, likewise, is not correct.

Another very popular explanation, probably the majority view, is that the restrainer refers to the law and order that came out of the Roman system of government. Roman rule was evil in many ways, but it did preserve a certain amount of law and order. Others expand this view to say that government or the power of the state in general restrains evil (cf. Rom. 13:1–5). Proponents of this view visualize the removal of law and order in the tribulation period with the result that restraint of evil is taken away. They believe that the Antichrist will be revealed then and sin will be brought out into the open.

But this explanation is also inadequate for two main reasons. First, human government is not stronger than Satan. Whatever or whoever the restrainer is must be stronger than Satan because it holds back his program from coming on the world scene. In Scripture, Satan is pictured as controlling, influencing, and deceiving the nations. Second, while the day of the Lord is a very evil period, it will be a time of rigid, super-strong government. There will be regimentation in that day such as we in America have never known. A government permit, what we might call the "tribulation trade-mark," will be required to go to the grocery store and buy and also to sell (Rev. 13:16–18). Government will not be removed in the tribulation. On the contrary, human government will reach its zenith of authority and power during this time.

For these reasons, this explanation does not seem to fit the passage either. Some of the other views of the identity of the restrainer are Michael the archangel, the preaching of the gospel, and even the apostle Paul. Concerning this issue, St. Augustine transparently said, "I frankly confess I do not know what he means." While we can sympathize with Augustine, there is one key question that points unmistakably to the identity of the restrainer.

Who, after all, really restrains sin and Satan? The answer found in the Bible is that God is the one who restrains sin. Genesis 6:3 declares that the Spirit of God was restraining sin in the days of Noah. It was predicted that instead of striving with sin, God would judge it in the flood.

The book of Job records that Satan wanted to afflict Job, but God had built an impenetrable hedge about him. Satan testified that he was restrained by God from trying Job (Job 1:9–11). When Satan accused Job of serving God because God had been so good to him, God took down part of the hedge and permitted Satan to take away all of Job's property and all of his children in one day. He left Job only his wife and his own life. When the Lord called Satan's attention to Job's faithfulness in affliction, Satan said it was because God had preserved Job's health. Then God permitted Satan to afflict Job's body, but not to take his life. Satan then brought severe physical affliction on Job, and Job was in torment in his body (2:1–8). But in it all Satan could not go any further than God permitted him. Satan was restrained by God Himself.

No believer would be able to do any work for God if it were not for God's protecting hand. God is the one who restrains. He may use varying means, including the government, which maintains a certain amount of law and order. Yet in the end God provides protection for the Christian.

More specifically, in this present age the Holy Spirit provides protection. As revealed in Genesis 6:3, the Spirit strives with humans and opposes Satan, his program, and his hatred of the children of God. Also, this is the only view that adequately explains the change in gender in verses 6–7, which we noted above. The restrainer is both a power—"what is restraining him now," and a person—"he who now restrains." In Greek the word *pneuma* ("spirit") is neuter. But the Holy Spirit is also consistently referred to by the masculine pronoun "He," especially in John 14–16. This fits the language of 2 Thessalonians 2:6–7 very well.

Of course, this view raises the question, In what sense can the Holy Spirit be removed from the world? While the Holy Spirit has always been present on earth and worked in times past, on the day of Pentecost the Spirit came in a special way. Christ, who had always existed and was always present in the world, came into the world, was born of the Virgin Mary, and in a special sense left the world when He ascended back to heaven—even though He said, "Behold, I am with you always" (Matt. 28:20). So also the Spirit of God came in a unique way on the day of Pentecost and now indwells the church and is present in the world. The restraining ministry of the Spirit through the church will return to heaven at the rapture.

The most natural explanation of the removal of the restrainer is to identify this particular action with the time when Christ will come to take out His church. If the Holy Spirit indwells the church and the church is taken out of the world, then the Spirit will also be taken out of the world. This does not mean that He will not continue working in the world in some way; but it will mean a reversal of Pentecost. Just as the Spirit came on Pentecost suddenly and unexpectedly, so He will leave suddenly and unexpectedly when Christ takes the church out of the world. The Holy Spirit must be present on earth during the future tribulation to convict sinners of their need for salvation and bring them to faith in Christ, just as He does today. The convicting, drawing, and regenerating ministry of the Spirit is essential for anyone to be saved, both now and in the tribulation (cf. John 3:5; 16:7–11; 1 Cor. 12:3). But the Spirit's restraining ministry through the church will be taken out of the way at the rapture. Barnhouse provides an excellent summary of the identity of the restrainer:

Well, what is keeping the Antichrist from putting in his appearance on the world stage? *You* are! You and every other member of the body of Christ on earth. The presence of the church of Jesus Christ is the restraining force that refuses to allow the man of lawlessness to be revealed. True, it is the Holy Spirit who is the real restrainer. But as both 1 Corinthians 3:16 and 6:19 teach, the Holy Spirit indwells the believer. The believer's body is the temple of the Spirit of God. Put all believers together then, with the Holy Spirit indwelling each of us, and you have a formidable restraining force.

For when the church is removed at the rapture, the Holy Spirit goes with the church insofar as His restraining power is concerned. His work in this age of grace will be ended. Henceforth, during the Great Tribulation, the Holy Spirit will still be here on earth, of course—for how can you get rid of God?—but He will not be indwelling believers as He does now. Rather, he will revert to His Old Testament ministry of "coming upon" special people.[5]

The sudden removal of both the church and the Spirit from the world will release the world to sin as it never has before. The rapture will change everything. The presence of believers in the world exerts a powerful influence on this evil world. Christians who stand for civic righteousness and law and order will no longer be present exerting their influence. The salt and light will be suddenly, completely extracted from the earth. For the time being at least, there will be no one except unsaved people to run government. The net result will be that evil will erupt and expand unchecked beyond anything known in history. It will be like the removal of a huge dam. Evil will run amok. The world will be flooded, pounded, and inundated with evil of unimaginable scope and severity. The "mystery of lawlessness" (v. 7) is, of course, already working, but the Holy Spirit is now restraining sin until He is taken away at the translation of the church. When this occurs, "then the lawless one will be revealed, whom the Lord Jesus will kill with the breath of his mouth and bring to nothing by the appearance of his coming" (v. 8).

Swindoll describes the results of the removal of the restrainer:

When the church is "gathered together" and taken to be with Christ in the air, the salt and light will be withdrawn. Then every vestige of goodness will decay; every remnant of truth, unravel. It is at that time when the man of lawlessness will take center stage. Like cages in a zoo suddenly opened, so will it be when the Restrainer is taken out of the way and lawlessness runs wild and rampant in the streets. Ours is a day of grace in which sin, to a large degree, is restrained. It is a day when God does not deal directly with human sin. However, there will come a time when He will step on the scene to deal definitively with sin. And that will be a time of great destruction.[6]

THREE AGES IN 2 THESSALONIANS 2:3–8[7]

Present Age (Before the Rapture)	**The Age of Restraint**
Tribulation Age (After the Rapture)	**The Age of Rebellion**
Messianic Age (After the Second Coming)	**The Age of Revelation**

Three good reasons show why the day of the Lord and the tribulation time could not have begun in the time when the Thessalonians lived: first, the apostasy had not come; second, the man of sin had not been revealed; and, third, the Spirit of God had not been taken away. Those unfulfilled conditions are still true today. While there is certainly gushing apostasy in our midst, the man of sin has not been revealed, and the Holy Spirit has not been removed. All of this constitutes real evidence that the tribulation time has not come and that it cannot come until Christ comes and takes His church home to glory.

SEVEN POINTS IN FAVOR OF THE PRETRIBULATIONAL RAPTURE IN THE THESSALONIAN EPISTLES

1. The coming of the Lord is presented as an imminent event, that is, one that could occur at any moment (1 Thess. 1:10). No preceding signs for the rapture are given. This is consistent with the pretribulational rapture position and inconsistent with the other views.

2. Believers will be delivered from the coming wrath (1 Thess. 1:10). Believers are not appointed to wrath (1 Thess. 5:9). The wrath in this context is the fierce judgment on an evil world at the day of the Lord.

3. The order of events in 1 Thessalonians 4:13–18 (the rapture) and 5:1–9 (the day of the Lord) point toward a pretribulational rapture. The rapture comes chronologically before the day of the Lord or tribulation period.

4. The rapture is to bring comfort and encouragement (1 Thess. 4:18). If the pretribulational position is not true, the Thessalonians should have been rejoicing that their loved ones were deceased rather than weeping, because by dying they would be spared the horrors of the tribulation. Also, what comfort would there be in the rapture if believers must endure one-half, three-fourths, or all of the great tribulation before it occurs?

5. Believers are specifically omitted from the day of the Lord in 1 Thessalonians 5:1–6. Paul does not include himself and the believers in this event the way he does with the rapture in 4:13–18.

6. The agitation of the believers about supposedly being in the day of the Lord indicates that they did not expect to be in it (2 Thess. 2:2). If they had been taught by Paul that they would be in the day of the Lord, they would not be upset to hear they had entered it. It would have been what they expected.

7. The restrainer, who is the restraining influence of the Holy Spirit through the church, must be removed for the man of sin to be revealed and the man of sin must be revealed before the tribulation can begin. This means the church must be taken out before the tribulation (2 Thess. 2:5–7).

THE CHARACTER OF THE LAWLESS ONE (2:9–12)

2:9–12 The coming of the lawless one is by the activity of Satan with all power and false signs and wonders, and with all wicked deception for those who are perishing, because they refused to love the truth and so be saved. Therefore God sends them a strong delusion, so that they may believe what is false, in order that all may be condemned who did not believe the truth but had pleasure in unrighteousness.

The Scriptures teach that Satan works by imitation, counterfeit, and deception. He wants to be like God. As God has described in His Word that Christ and Christ alone can rule the world in peace and righteousness, and has proved the deity of Christ by the many miracles He performed, so this "lawless one" will be Satan's man even as Christ is God's Man. The Antichrist's arrival is called a *parousia* (coming) in 2:9, the same word that is used of Christ's coming in 2:1. In addition, Antichrist's appearance is called an *apokalupsis* ("revelation") three times (2:3, 6, 8, translated "revealed"), which is the same word used of Christ's second coming in 1:7. The coming of the Antichrist will be such a complete, clever parody of the coming of Christ that many will be drawn in by the demonic deception.

The Antichrist will be promoted in the world by the false prophet described in Revelation 13:11–18, and he will assume the role of a super-man. He will be put forward as the outstanding leader who can rescue the world from its difficulties and stop the chaos. His power will come from Satan himself and Satan will energize him to perform certain signs and lying wonders. Revelation 13:2 says, "And the beast that I saw was like a leopard; its feet were like a bear's, and its mouth was like a lion's mouth. And to it the dragon gave his power and his throne and great authority." The signs and wonders he will do by Satan's power will not be on the same plane as the miracles Christ performed, but he will be able to perform acts that are stupendous and supernatural. In stunned amazement, the world will say of him, "Who is like the beast?" (Rev. 13:4).

Verses 9–12 describe the way in which Satan will work to deceive the world. The Scriptures clearly teach that in that future day many will be deceived and will not receive Jesus Christ as their Savior. The Antichrist will come as a substitute in place of Christ, and people who resisted Christ and did not receive Him and were left behind at the rapture will flock in great numbers to follow this evil character. This will come to pass, of course, in the time of the great tribulation. All of this is declared to be a judgment from God. People will be deceived and perish "because they refused to love the truth and so be saved." The result will be that "God sends them a strong delusion, so that they may believe what is false." But how can God delude a person? The answer is given in the context.

First, it is clear that those who are deceived had opportunity to receive Christ, but they did not do it. There seems to be a principle of divine justice here that when a person turns away from the truth, God allows that one to be led off into error. So often when people depart from the truth it is because they have resisted the Spirit of God as He sought to lead them into the knowledge of the Word of God. So it will be in that day. Those who have turned away from Christ will turn instead to this false leader and thus will believe a lie instead of believing the truth.

Some understand from verse 11 that if a person in this present age of grace hears the gospel and does not receive Christ as his Savior, then when Christ comes and takes His church home to glory that person will find it impossible to be saved after the church is raptured. It is unlikely that a person who rejects Christ in this day of grace will turn to Him in that awful period of tribulation. It will not get easier to turn to Christ; it will be much more difficult. However, the usual principle of Scripture is that while there is life there is hope.

Thus it is possible, though very improbable, that a person who has heard the gospel in this present age of grace will come to Christ after the rapture. But we must remember the context of this passage. It is focused on people who reject Christ during the tribulation and receive Antichrist, not on people who rejected Christ before the rapture. The Scriptures definitely teach that after the church is gone, God will send strong delusion to those who do not believe. God will judge their hearts, and if they deliberately turn away from the truth He will permit them to believe a lie. They will honor the man of lawlessness as their god and king, instead of acknowledging the Lord Jesus Christ. The result will be "that all may be condemned who did not believe the truth but had pleasure in unrighteousness" (v. 12).

The awful destiny of those who turn away from the Lord Jesus Christ is presented in verse 12 so clearly. Sadly, many today will not receive Christ. They are indifferent and turn away without trusting Him. Christians often fail to realize how desperate is the condition of one who hears the gospel and turns away. The choice is not an unimportant alternative. People are actually determining their eternal destiny. Those who turn from Christ find themselves in a path of total hopelessness. They are headed, as the Scriptures make very clear, into eternal punishment.

This solemn truth should give us a sense of the urgency of our day to tell people about Christ. The great majority of people who are within the sound of the gospel today will not heed and turn to Christ. They will flock after this false leader and, instead of believing in Christ in that dreadful time of the tribulation, they will believe a lie and rush headlong to their eternal damnation. But in this day of grace Christians have a real commission. The climactic days of the day of the Lord will not come until Christ comes for us first. While we wait we certainly should be challenged by the Lord to give our hearts and lives to Him. As God enables us and gives opportunity to proclaim the gospel, the message should be sent forth that Christ loves those who are lost and died for them, that He is able to save them if they will come to Him. Christians need not fear the coming of this tribulation time, for we have the hope of His imminent return.

Believers will have trouble in this world and some have endured awful trials. There have been tens of thousands of martyrs in our generation. But this is not the day of the Lord; this is not the time of tribulation. This is still the day of grace. God is still waiting for lost men and women to come to Him. One of these days the last soul will be added to the church, and the church—the body of Christ—will be complete. When that last one accepts the Lord Jesus, at that very moment the Lord will come for His church, and the completed body of Christ will be caught up to be with the Lord. Then will follow, as the Scriptures make plain, this dreadful period described as the day of the Lord—the time when God's judgments will be poured out on an unbelieving world.

The obvious lesson from this portion of Scripture is that we should examine our own hearts. Have we really trusted Christ? Have we been born again through faith in Him? If you have not trusted in Him before, now is the time to put your faith in Him. If you take this step, you can look forward with every other Christian to the coming of the Lord. That is our hope. We also learn from this passage that God's timetable is right on schedule. He has a program that He will bring to pass in His time. "History is not a random series of meaningless events. It is rather a succession of periods and happenings which are under the sovereign rule of God, who is the God of history."[8]

The first event in His chain of end-time events—the trigger for it all—will be the rapture of the church and the removal of the restrainer. After that the world will plunge into darkness of the day of the Lord as the apostasy fully emerges and the Antichrist enters the spotlight. But we need not fear the coming of the day of the Lord, for when that day comes on earth we will be with the Lord in glory.

NOTES

1. Charles R. Swindoll, *Steadfast Christianity: A Study of Second Thessalonians,* Bible Study Guide (Anaheim, CA: Insight for Living, 1986), 23.

2. D. Edmond Hiebert, *1 and 2 Thessalonians* (Chicago: Moody, 1971), 331.

3. Swindoll, *Steadfast Christianity,* 24.

4. Warren W. Wiersbe, *The Bible Exposition Commentary: An Exposition of the New Testament,* vol. 2 (Wheaton, IL: Victor, 1989), 197.

5. Donald Grey Barnhouse, *Thessalonians: An Expositional Commentary* (Grand Rapids: Zondervan, 1977), 99–100.

6. Swindoll, *Steadfast Christianity,* 25.

7. John Stott, *The Gospel and the End of Time: The Message of 1 and 2 Thessalonians* (Downers Grove, IL: InterVarsity, 1991), 173.

8. Ibid., 173.

9

Chosen to Salvation
2 Thessalonians 2:13–17

Having laid before the Thessalonians the wonderful hope of the coming of the Lord in the future, Paul then addressed the immediate task of living for God in the present. While waiting for Christ to come for His church, believers have a task to perform, a life to live, a testimony to give. These things should be their present concern.

CHOSEN FROM THE BEGINNING
THROUGH THE GOSPEL (2:13–14)

2:13–14 But we ought always to give thanks to God for you, brothers beloved by the Lord, because God chose you as the first-fruits to be saved, through sanctification by the Spirit and belief in the truth. To this he called you through our gospel, so that you may obtain the glory of our Lord Jesus Christ.

Second Thessalonians 2:13–17 has been called "a system of theology in miniature." It is a marvelously comprehensive statement of God's saving purposes. In verse 13, Paul gave thanks to the Lord for having chosen these Thessalonian Christians for salvation. The revelation that is stated here so simply is one of the most profound doctrines of the entire Word of God. In fact, in one sense the doctrine of salvation is more profound than the subject of the Lord's second coming. Our salvation did not originate in human choice. God willed our salvation long before we ever came into existence. This divine choice was based on divine love and divine determination. Paul gave thanks because they were "brothers beloved by the Lord."

One of the great truths of Scripture is that before we ever loved the Lord,

He loved us. This is stated in the familiar text of John 3:16, "For God so loved the world." Some would like to make these words read "God so loved the elect." God does love the elect, but that is not what the text says. God loved the world. He loved the unsaved. He loved them all. That is why He gave His Son. The love of God is mentioned often in Scripture. First John 4:10 states, "In this is love, not that we have loved God but that he loved us and sent his Son to be the propitiation for our sins."

Likewise, out of God's heart of love there was a divine decision in eternity past which is referred to here as our being chosen. The original act in our salvation was with God, not with us. God set His distinguishing love on the elect before they were ever born. God made the first move. When God chose us to salvation, He did not choose us because we were lovely or because He saw something in us that He did not see in others. Instead He chose us because He loved us.

A mystery is associated with God's choosing us for salvation that none of us can ever completely fathom. But the glorious fact is that He set His love on us. Ephesians 1:4 describes this choice this way: "even as he chose us in him before the foundation of the world, that we should be holy and blameless before him. In love . . ." The precious truth is that God chose us (John 6:37, 44; 15:16). This is the occasion of the apostle's thanksgiving in verse 13.

The testimony of the Thessalonians showed clearly that they were the chosen ones of God. In 1 Thessalonians 1:4 Paul had written earlier, "For we know, brothers loved by God, that he has chosen you." So here again these young believers at Thessalonica were reminded of God's grace in their election and salvation.

The process by which God chose these Christians at Thessalonica, and how they were brought to salvation, is revealed at the end of verse 13: "through sanctification by the Spirit and belief in the truth." Sanctification means to be *set apart as holy to God*. How has God sanctified those who once were bound for eternal punishment, were without God, without hope, and under His wrath? How is it possible to take such people and sanctify them by the Holy Spirit?

Christ spoke of this tremendous process in John 16. He was discussing with His disciples the need for His going away. The disciples did not want Him to go away, so He told them:

> Nevertheless, I tell you the truth: it is to your advantage that I go away, for if I do not go away, the Helper will not come to you. But if I go, I will send him to you. And when he comes, he will convict the world concerning sin and righteousness and judgment: concerning sin, because they do not believe in me; concerning righteousness, because I go to the Father, and you will see me no longer; concerning judgment, because the ruler of this world is judged. (vv. 7–11)

These significant verses teach that when a person is coming to Christ there must be a work of the Spirit in his heart before he can come. That is the convicting work of the Holy Spirit. The Spirit awakens and enables a person lost in sin to understand the truth of the gospel. The ministry of the Spirit is not to convict of sins (plural), or to make us realize what awful sinners we are. That may be a part of the process, but that is not the point. What the Spirit desires to impress on an unsaved person is the one fact that he is not saved because he has not believed. This is the sin of unbelief, defined in verse 9, "concerning sin, because they do not believe in me." The Holy Spirit must bring a person to the place where he realizes that the one obstacle standing between him being lost forever and gaining eternal salvation is lack of faith in Christ. One is ultimately lost because he or she has not trusted Christ. But salvation comes as a result of simply trusting in the Savior.

The passage explains the ministry of the Spirit further: "concerning righteousness, because I go to the Father, and you will see me no longer" (John 16:10). While Christ was on earth He was the living embodiment of righteousness. As people studied His life and saw what He did, they beheld the righteousness of God in action. But Christ was not here to tell us about righteousness. Unsaved people must be instructed on the subject of righteousness by the Spirit of God. They must learn, of course, that God is righteous. But most of all they need to know that God is able to give righteousness, to justify, to declare righteous, those who are willing to trust in Christ. God bestows a justification, a righteousness, a right standing with Him, that is by faith—the gift of God, purchased for us by Christ on the cross. When a person trusts in Christ he is indeed righteous. The ministry of the Spirit makes this truth plain.

The passage in John 16 speaks also of the fact that "the ruler of this world is judged." This is a description of Christ's victory over Satan at the cross. Because of Jesus' death on the cross, Satan is now judged. Satan has been defeated by the death of Christ, and Satan's doom is assured. Behind this pre-salvation aspect of sanctification is the work of the Spirit in bringing a person to the place where he sees that he can be saved by simply trusting in Jesus Christ. When a person trusts in Christ, then the work of sanctification begins. First, there is the work of regeneration. Christ told Nicodemus, "You must be born again" (John 3:7); "unless one is born of water and the Spirit, he cannot enter the kingdom of God" (John 3:5). The person who once was lost and spiritually dead now becomes alive and receives a new nature in Christ. As such he is made fit to be set apart as holy to God.

Another phase of the Holy Spirit's sanctifying work is His ministry as He comes to indwell us. In 1 Corinthians 6, Paul reminded the worldly Corinthians that if they were really saved their bodies were the temples of God: "Or do you not know that your body is a temple of the Holy Spirit within you, whom you have from God? You are not your own, for you were bought with a price. So glorify God in your body" (1 Cor. 6:19). In other words, every Christian is a sanctuary of God in whom God has seen fit to take up His dwelling place. This is a marvelous truth and a part of the sanctifying work of the Holy Spirit as He sets us apart as His own sanctuary.

Because of the Holy Spirit's indwelling presence in Christians, they are sealed by the Spirit. His very presence is God's seal, God's token of ownership and security in Christ. In Ephesians 4:30 the exhortation is given, "And do not grieve the Holy Spirit of God, by whom you were sealed for the day of redemption." The day of redemption is the day of believers' resurrection, the day when their bodies will be redeemed. As far as our souls are concerned, we are redeemed right now, but our bodies are not yet redeemed. According to the Scriptures, the presence of the Spirit is God's token to us, His promise that we will be saved completely and transformed on that day when our bodies are redeemed.

In 1 Corinthians 12:13, still another aspect of the Spirit's sanctifying work is revealed: "For in one Spirit we were all baptized into one body—Jews or Greeks, slaves or free—and all were made to drink of one Spirit." The very moment one is saved, the Holy Spirit takes that person out of his position in Adam—in sin and under condemnation—and places him in Christ, that is, in the body of Christ, so that he is a living part of the organism we call the true church. This is also part of the sanctifying work of the Spirit. We are set apart as belonging to God. In addition to all that God provides for the individual in Christ in salvation, there is the ongoing possibility of being filled by the Spirit as we yield ourselves to Him. The Holy Spirit works in us the divine character that God has ordained, and the fruit of the Spirit—the love, the joy, the peace, etc. (cf. Gal. 5:22–23)—become our portion. Paul's thanksgiving for the Thessalonian Christians was because God had chosen them to salvation through sanctification of the Spirit.

This was the third time in his two letters that Paul had focused on the sanctification of the Thessalonians. In 1 Thessalonians 4:3–8, he presented the progressive, ongoing sanctification that the Spirit accomplishes in our lives in setting us apart more and more as we yield to His power. The final, future aspect of sanctification, when believers will be perfectly set apart to the Lord, was mentioned in 1 Thessalonians 5:23: "Now may the God of peace himself sanctify you completely."

THREE ASPECTS OF SANCTIFICATION IN THE THESSALONIAN EPISTLES

1. Preparatory Sanctification (2 Thess. 2:13)

2. Progressive Sanctification (1 Thess. 4:3)

3. Perfect Sanctification (1 Thess. 5:23)

The last part of verse 13 brings out another great truth: "through sanctification by the Spirit and belief in the truth." This verse has a very significant order. It begins with God and the process is carried through by the Holy Spirit. The believer's part is stated simply; it is through "belief in the truth." On our part, salvation and sanctification come because we are willing to trust in the Savior. This is a wonderful truth. Salvation from the Lord delivers us from legalism or any kind of works-based salvation. This makes clear that it is impossible to build a ladder to heaven by some sort of good works, religion, or church ordinances. There is a proper place for works, but they are not the way of salvation (Eph. 2:8–10). Works are the fruit of salvation, not the root. They pertain to the Christian life and testimony, but salvation is something God has to do for us and that we receive by faith alone.

The Thessalonians were called to this glorious salvation: "To this he called you through our gospel, so that you may obtain the glory of our Lord Jesus Christ" (v. 14). They were called by the gospel, the means that God used to bring about the fulfillment of His choice, by the sanctifying work of the Spirit, and by their belief in the truth. We are reminded again how the apostle Paul is jealous for the gospel. In Galatians he pronounced a curse on anyone who does not preach the true gospel. He believed in putting the gospel first. In 1 Corinthians 15:1–4 he told the Corinthians that when he came to them he declared to them the gospel, which is "that Christ died for our sins in accordance with the Scriptures, that he was buried, that he was raised on the third day in accordance with the Scriptures."

One of the tragedies of Christianity in our modern day is that there is so little clear preaching of the gospel. What was the good news, the message that led these Thessalonian believers to know Jesus Christ as their Savior? The good news was that Christ, the Son of God, had come and had died on the cross for the sins of the whole world. The good news was that though He was buried, He was raised the third day in victory over the grave in newness of life, evidence that He is indeed the very Son of God. His resurrection was a demonstration of the power of God and of the deity of Christ's own person. It was evidence of the fact that when He died, He had accomplished what only an infinite person could accomplish—our eternal and infinite redemption. This is the true gospel.

As Paul wrote this letter, he thought back to the time when he had told the believers at Thessalonica these truths, and how they had believed them. Through believing the gospel, they had become gloriously and wonderfully saved. But Paul also took a look at the future, "so that you may obtain the glory of our Lord Jesus Christ" (v. 14). We need to remember that the Thessalonians were in great affliction. They were going through real persecution. As Paul lifted up their eyes beyond their circumstances, he reminded them that they were bound for the glory of the Lord Jesus Christ. The Scriptures declare plainly that before God is through with us, every one of us will be perfectly glorious. We are trophies of God's grace. Throughout eternity the church will be singled out as the example of what the grace of God can do by taking poor, hell-bound sinners and transforming them to be His holy saints, to be conformed to the image of Christ. That is glory. Believers have many imperfections now, but when God completes His work, the church will be a perfect bride for the Lord Jesus. That is the glory ahead.

EXHORTATION TO STAND FAST (2:15–17)

2:15–17 So then, brothers, stand firm and hold to the traditions that you were taught by us, either by our spoken word or by our letter. Now may our Lord Jesus Christ himself, and God our Father, who loved us and gave us eternal comfort and good hope through grace, comfort your hearts and establish them in every good work and word.

On the basis of the wonderful truths and tokens of what God had done for Paul's readers, Paul exhorted them to "stand firm." The Thessalonians needed this word, as do we today, because a natural tendency in the Christian heart is to backslide. Against this we must stand firm. The Thessalonians were facing tough times: persecution, suffering, and false teaching. Strong currents were threatening to knock them down. Likewise, today there are all kinds of currents in our ungodly culture that will sweep us downstream if we lose our spiritual footing. We must stand firm by clinging to what is solid and secure, and "hold on" to the Word of God.

The word for "traditions" (*paradoseis*) means "that which is given alongside or the things handed on." This does not refer to human or church traditions devised by people (as in Mark 7:3–9 and Col. 2:8). Ryrie says, "The word *traditions* does not mean things which men have made up but merely something which has been passed on from one to another and which was received in the first place from God Himself."[1] First Corinthians 11:2 says, "Now I commend you because you remember me in everything and maintain the traditions even as I delivered them to you." In 2 Thessalonians 3:6, Paul again referred to "the tradition that you received from us." The reference in 2:15 to these traditions "that you were taught by us, either by our spoken word or by our letter" is probably a reference back to 1 Thessalonians. The message they had received came from God. Today, the apostolic traditions are contained in the Scriptures. No more of these "traditions" are being given today. This revelation has ceased since there are no more apostles (Eph. 2:20).

However, we do have teachers and preachers today who mine out the treasures of Scripture to build up other believers by applying it to life. Men of God down through church history have studied the Bible and faithfully expounded what it teaches. The commentaries they have written are not inspired, and they are not infallible; however, many expositors are very faithful in their exposition of the Scriptures. The teaching that accompanies the written Word, that is "given alongside," should be held fast by Christians even though none but the teachings of the apostles as contained in the Scriptures are infallible.

How we can thank God for faithful teachers and preachers of the Word! How much their teaching has contributed to the church! Paul said in reference to such teaching, "Hold on to it." The tendency in our day is always to be looking for something new and different. We need to realize that truth is not new. As H. A. Ironside used to say, "What is new is not true, and what is true is not new." In other words, it is the old truth that is true. Of course, we may find truths that are new to us. One can read the Bible and discover a new thought, only to find that others long ago had already seen the same truth. This was new truth to the individual even though it was old truth. Of course, we should endeavor to learn more of the Scriptures, but we should also hold on to the traditions, the things we have been taught.

In verses 16–17, Paul closed this section with a prayer. This portion of Scripture serves as a reminder of the place of prayer and how Christians need to let God have His way in their prayer life. The prayer is addressed to the Father and to the Lord Jesus Christ. The deity of Christ is highlighted in verse 16. John Stott observes:

> But this time he startles us by even putting the Son before the Father. It is amazing enough, within twenty years of the resurrection, that Paul should have bracketed Jesus Christ with God; it is yet more amazing that he now brackets God with Jesus Christ. He also goes on, in spite of the plurality of the subject (Father and Son), to use the singular reflexive *who* and the singular verbs *loved* and *gave*. Paul is evidently quite clear, at least in the practice of prayer if not yet in theological formulation, about the equality and the unity of the Father and the Son.[2]

This verse tells us how Jesus and the Father have loved us and how they have given us "eternal comfort and good hope through grace." On the basis of the prospect before them, the Thessalonians were to comfort their hearts and to be established in "every good work and word." In other words, their Christian life and testimony consisted in what they said and did in everyday life.

Paul prayed that they would be established, that is, be firm and faithful in the tasks God had given them. As we in our day face the challenge of our own lives may these truths be not only for the Thessalonian church, but may they also grip our hearts. May we thank God that He chose us. May we thank Him for the sanctifying work of the Holy Spirit that drew us to Him and set us apart. May we thank Him that someone gave us the gospel and that into our hearts there came faith in the Word of God and in the gospel of our Lord Jesus Christ. Let us thank God for all He has done to us and for us, and let us thank Him that now our destiny is to have the glory of our Lord and Savior Jesus Christ.

NOTES

1. Charles Caldwell Ryrie, *First and Second Thessalonians,* Everyman's Bible Commentary (Chicago: Moody, 1959), 117.
2. John Stott, *The Gospel & the End of Time: The Message of 1 &2 Thessalonians* (Downers Grove, IL: InterVarsity Press, 1991), 179.

10 Serving and Waiting
2 Thessalonians 3:1–18

In the closing portion of 2 Thessalonians 2, a tremendous revelation of the riches of our wonderful salvation was given—that God chose us in eternity past and saved us through the hearing and believing of the gospel message as it was preached. Because of this, we have glory ahead. On the basis of these truths, Paul exhorted the believers at Thessalonica to stand fast and to continue in their Christian life and testimony.

EXHORTATION TO PRAY (3:1–5)

3:1–4 Finally, brothers, pray for us, that the word of the Lord may speed ahead and be honored, as happened among you, and that we may be delivered from wicked and evil men. For not all have faith. But the Lord is faithful. He will establish you and guard you against the evil one. And we have confidence in the Lord about you, that you are doing and will do the things that we command.

The third chapter of this epistle presents some of the privileges and responsibilities that belong to a true believer in any age. This first exhortation is a reminder that all of us need prayer. The Thessalonians were facing difficulties and troubles. Some of them were probably in danger of their lives because of their testimony for Jesus Christ. In their affliction Paul was trying to help and comfort them by reminding them of the great verities of the faith. At the same time, he addressed their continued obligation to serve the Lord. Experiencing trials in life does not exempt us from the responsibility to serve the Lord and others.

While Paul was writing to the Thessalonians about their troubles and the Lord's comfort and help for them, he had been reticent to talk about his own troubles. But Paul, too, was having his share of difficulties. The ministry committed to him was a very lonely one: to go from place to place, frequently coming into a strange city where not one person would welcome him. He was not entertained in the best hotels, nor was there any impressive honorarium for him in recognition of his services. He had to find his own way, arrange for his public meetings, and somehow try to bear a faithful, consistent testimony for Christ. Apart from fellowship with the Lord, Paul's ministry was a difficult and solitary task and one in which there were many discouragements. A few years later, Paul chronicled his trials:

> with far greater labors, far more imprisonments, with countless beatings, and often near death. Five times I received at the hands of the Jews the forty lashes less one. Three times I was beaten with rods. Once I was stoned. Three times I was shipwrecked; a night and a day I was adrift at sea; on frequent journeys, in danger from rivers, danger from robbers, danger from my own people, danger from Gentiles, danger in the city, danger in the wilderness, danger at sea, danger from false brothers; in toil and hardship, through many a sleepless night, in hunger and thirst, often without food, in cold and exposure. And, apart from other things, there is the daily pressure on me of my anxiety for all the churches. (2 Cor. 11:23–28)

With this as a background, without complaining or saying very much about it, Paul asked the church at Thessalonica to pray for him. In effect, he was saying, "Don't forget that I need your prayers, too. You are not the only ones who are in trouble." This was sound advice to the Thessalonians. One of the best ways for you to be aided in dealing with your own burden is to help bear someone else's burden. If you realize that others have needs too, as you pray for them it will make your own load lighter.

Paul asked his readers to "pray for us, that the word of the Lord may speed ahead and be honored, as happened among you." The average layperson does not realize how much a minister of the gospel depends on the prayers of God's people. Whenever an evangelist or a Bible teacher attempts to expound the Word of God, he is not only contending against failure on the part of those who listen, but against the unseen powers of darkness. He is engaging in a cosmic spiritual war. All the powers of hell are arrayed against him. Whenever one tries to do something for the Lord, a spiritual battle ensues.

No one can win the battle alone. No preacher who has been used of God was not supported by God's people in prayer. Even an ordinary person without extraordinary gifts can accomplish much if God's people pray for him or her. Paul was a great leader, and God had given him wonderful spiritual gifts, had marvelously called him to serve Him, and had used him. But Paul was first to confess, "I cannot do it alone. I need your prayers." Paul, the great apostle, was willing to humbly ask new Christians to pray for him. Behind every victory for the Word of God there must be a victory in prayer. When calling on a certain college president years ago, I asked how things were going. His reply was, "We are going forward on our knees." That was the right answer. In the Lord's work, if we are not on our knees, progress does not amount to much. It must be progress in prayer.

In all our labor for the Lord, we must pray. God has not called everyone to be a great preacher, teacher, or leader. Some could not teach a Sunday school class and do a good job of it. They just do not have the gifts. On the other hand, it is surprising what God can do with a person who is willing. Some have more gifts than they realize and are just too timid to use them. But every Christian can pray.

Prayer is not a spiritual gift given only to some. Prayer is the privilege of every child of God. God has given us the ability of speech, and He has also given us the privilege to talk to Him on our knees. The marvelous thing about prayer is that every Christian is on the same level. Some believers may know more than others, but in the work of prayer each believer comes to God in the name of Christ. What more could anyone desire than that? The small child and the mature saint have equal access to the throne of grace. In writing to the Thessalonians who were young Christians and were perhaps overly occupied with their own needs, Paul urged them to pray.

Prayer is effective in overcoming opposition, and so Paul added, "and that we may be delivered from wicked and evil men. For not all have faith" (v. 2). Sometimes in the Lord's work we experience opposition and hindrances. If we were in many parts of the world today, we would know what it is to endure the opposition of those who are hostile to Christ. We would realize something of how Satan can use human beings to hinder the preaching of the gospel. This kind of opposition, however, is not limited to dark corners of the world. It is becoming more common almost daily here in the United States and other Western nations in one form or another. Even here believers sometimes risk their advancement in business, and possibly their lives, in taking a bold stand for the gospel. We need divine deliverance as we preach the Word, not only from satanic power but also from human instruments who are under the control of Satan. Our weapon is prayer.

How often we need to come back to the statement in Ephesians 6:12, "For we do not wrestle against flesh and blood, but against the rulers, against the authorities, against the cosmic powers over this present darkness, against the spiritual forces of evil in the heavenly places." Our battle is against the demonic forces of Satan that operate behind the scenes. That is the real battle, and that is why in Ephesians 6:18 we are exhorted to be "praying at all times in the Spirit, with all prayer and supplication." This victory is possible only through prayer. In modern warfare the nation with air superiority will experience victory. Likewise, in spiritual warfare the person who controls the air through prayer will win the spiritual war.

This prayer is, first, for the Word of God and its power, and then prayer for deliverance from ungodly opponents. Paul's focus was not on his own problems but on the effectiveness of his ministry for the Lord. In Ephesians 6:18b–20, Paul again asked prayer for success in his ministry: "To that end keep alert with all perseverance, making supplication for all the saints, and also for me, that words may be given to me in opening my mouth boldly to proclaim the mystery of the gospel, for which I am an ambassador in chains, that I may declare it boldly, as I ought to speak." The success of God's work and word was Paul's passion.

A word of assurance follows in 2 Thessalonians 3:3: "But the Lord is faithful. He will establish you and guard you against the evil one." Christians are often unfaithful to their promises and commitments. But we can depend on God; He is faithful. One thing we learn through the various experiences of life is that, though we may be unfaithful, God is never unfaithful. We can always depend on God to do what He has promised to do: "He who calls you is faithful; he will surely do it" (1 Thess. 5:24). Paul reminded the Thessalonians again that God is faithful to hear and answer prayer, and will guard us against Satan's attacks. This is another way of expressing the truth of Romans 8:28, "for those who love God all things work together for good." Paul was reminding the Thessalonians that even in their trials and tribulations God would faithfully work things out for their good and to His glory.

Paul anticipated their faithfulness in prayer in verse 4. Can others depend on us to do the right things? Can we be counted on? When the call to duty, or worship, or prayer comes to us, are we in our place? As he wrote the Thessalonian believers, Paul had confidence that they would be faithful. May others have that confidence in us.

3:5 May the Lord direct your hearts to the love of God and to the steadfastness of Christ.

Here Paul pointed his readers in a different direction. Verse 5 is just a short phrase, but it says much. We are in a world that has so many bids for our affection. The issue comes up as to what is really first, God or our families and loved ones. This is not always easy to answer. Then there is the enticement of money. The Scriptures warn us against the love of money (cf. 1 Tim. 6:9–10). One does not have to be rich to love money. One can be very poor and still have this problem. The temptation to love things and the power to do what money can do is constant. No one is exempt from the clutches of greed. Another lure is the love of the world, the love of its pleasures, comforts, and appearance. It is dangerous for Christians to set their hearts on something—anything—other than the Lord.

Recognizing this constant temptation, Paul told the Thessalonians, in the midst of their trials and troubles, and service for the Lord, not to forget to love Him. This is one of the most important things in life. The Lord is more interested in our hearts than He is in what we do, what we give, or what we say. Most of all He wants our love. If He has our love, everything else will fall in line. This is why Paul exhorted them, "direct your hearts to the love of God."

Along with love, the Thessalonians needed "the steadfastness [patience] of Christ." This refers to our patient waiting for Christ at His coming. Once again Paul set before them the goal of the Christian expectation. He did not say, "Patiently wait for the day of the Lord." Nor did he say, "Patiently wait until the time of tribulation comes." That is not the point. He said, "Patiently wait for the Lord," for the One who will rapture His church someday. That is our expectation, and that is our hope.

HOW TO WAIT FOR THE LORD (3:6–12)

3:6–10 Now we command you, brothers, in the name of our Lord Jesus Christ, that you keep away from any brother who is walking in idleness and not in accord with the tradition that you received from us. For you yourselves know how you ought to imitate us, because we were not idle when we were with you, nor did we eat anyone's bread without paying for it, but with toil and labor we worked night and day, that we might not be a burden to any of you. It was not because we do not have that right, but to give you in ourselves an example to imitate. For even when we were with you, we would give you this command: If anyone is not willing to work, let him not eat.

In these verses Paul gave his readers an extremely clear and practical list of things that Christians should pay attention to as they are waiting for the Lord. Frequently in this epistle we have seen that a true attitude of expectation regarding the Lord's coming is to affect our daily lives. In other words, God did not intend for us, after we have learned the precious truth that Christ is coming back, to sit with starry eyes and folded hands and look up to the heavens. God wants us to face the challenge of each day, recognizing that it might be the last day before Christ comes. We should make every day count for the Lord. Christ should be first in the day. We should do the things that He wants us to do.

Paul directed his exhortations to those in Thessalonica who were "walking in idleness" (v. 6)—not working, but expecting others to feed them. This is an illustration of the fact that as Christians, our lives should have order. Some in the early church, just as in modern times, had a tendency to go off into some sort of abnormal experience instead of being orderly and disciplined in their lives. The Thessalonians were told to withdraw from such brothers and sisters, because order and reverence should characterize the Christian's life. There should be a respectful attitude toward things of God. This was Paul's own standard (v. 7). He worked hard when he was in Thessalonica and paid his own way by making tents.

The key thought in 2 Thessalonians 3:6–15 is "work," "labor," or "toil." These words appear a total of six times and translate three different Greek words, all of which refer to work. In contrast, the word translated "idle" means disorderly, out of step, going one's own way. Each chapter in 2 Thessalonians deals with a different group that was troubling the church. Chapter 1 deals with persecutors, chapter 2 deals with false teachers, and chapter 3 focuses on idle, undisciplined believers. It seems that there were some in this Thessalonian church who had this lazy attitude. They said, "Since the Lord is coming, there is no use getting a job, or trying to earn our bread. I will eat at your house as long as you have food, and if you run out we will go to someone else. Because the Lord is coming we need not work." Once in a while we find people who are just about as impractical as that in relation to the Lord's coming.

But Paul said, "That is not what I taught you. While I was among you, I earned my own living in order to provide the necessities of my life. I was not dependent on you. I paid my own way. I provided my own food. Now I have set you an example. You should be providing for your own things. You should not be living at the expense of others."

Here is the proper Christian standard. But some have adopted the philosophy that the world owes them a living. This is not found in the Bible. The attitude of the Bible is that the world owes the Christian nothing, but that we owe the world something. We have something to give to the world. This does not mean that Christians should be opposed to any true social program that helps others. But we are not to take the attitude that the world owes us a living. The provision for God's people, according to Scripture, is a four-letter word—WORK.

Paul laid down the principle in verse 10: "If anyone is not willing to work, let him not eat." It does not say, "If one cannot work," but, "If anyone is not willing to work." Some are unable to work and provide fully for their own needs, and the church needs to meet their needs willingly and graciously. But those who will not work are not to eat. That was a simple method of getting folks to work. If they did not eat, they had to do something. Paul had already dealt with this issue twice before (1 Thess. 4:11–12; 5:14), but apparently the idlers did not listen to the teaching in the first letter, so he emphasized it here in more detail and more forcefully. He refused to let them ignore him.

3:11–12 For we hear that some among you walk in idleness, not busy at work, but busybodies. Now such persons we command and encourage in the Lord Jesus Christ to do their work quietly and to earn their own living.

The fact that these people were idle had led them into all sorts of difficulty. Idleness is fertile ground in which the devil can sow seeds.

Usually the type of person who does not mind his own business is idle because he is too busy trying to take care of someone else's business—minding everyone's business but his own. That was true in the Thessalonian church. Wiersbe notes, "They had time on their hands and gossip on their lips and they defended themselves by saying—the Lord is coming."[1] Paul's exhortation was strong and straightforward: "Get busy. Earn an honest living. Pay your own way. Take care of yourself. You will not have time, then, to be interfering with other people's business and making a nuisance of yourself in the church of God." Paul also told them to work "quietly," that is, without making a big noise about it. Just quietly do the right thing, provide your own livelihood, and eat your own bread. Do not sponge off of the charity of others. Do not expect someone else to feed you.

COMMAND TO CONTINUE IN WELL-DOING (3:13–15)

3:13–15 As for you, brothers, do not grow weary in doing good. If anyone does not obey what we say in this letter, take note of that person, and have nothing to do with him, that he may be ashamed. Do not regard him as an enemy, but warn him as a brother.

Paul also had a positive word of exhortation for those who had been doing the right thing: stay with it. Sometimes we can "grow weary of doing good" (Gal. 6:9) in the sense that we are physically tired. There is nothing immoral about that. But Paul meant we should not be weary in the sense that we want to quit doing good. The temptation when we see others who are not doing the right thing is to say, "What's the use? I'm trying to do the right thing and no one else is. I think I'll quit." Do you ever feel like that? Apparently some in the Thessalonian church were having a little trouble along that line, so Paul said, in essence, "Keep on being faithful in the task God has given you."

Further, Paul gave advice concerning fellowship with those in the church who were disobedient: "Take note of that person, and have nothing to do with him, that he may be ashamed" (v. 14). This may be a difficult verse for us to apply today. Some Christians have overworked it to the point where they think there is no one good enough for them. That is a sad attitude, too. But on the other hand the verse teaches that we should not pick as our associates and friends those who despise and disobey the Word of God.

Much depends on our friendships. Young people as well as those who are older should choose friends among Christian people who love the Lord. Such a choice will save a lot of temptation and keep them away from many heartaches and headaches. It is a good idea for young people to limit their

155

close social engagements to those who are Christians and love the Lord. This may reduce the number of friends, but the friendships that remain will mean something and will be worthwhile. This may save a person from the heartache of a marriage that is not in the will of the Lord, for example.

The issue at hand was that these disobedient believers were not listening to the Word of God. Paul was claiming that this letter was the Word of God, is to be heeded as a command of God. Fellowship is with those who are in obedience to the Word and who are living according to its standards.

Then Paul added a word of caution in verse 15: "Do not regard him as an enemy, but warn him as a brother." In other words, do not walk around with a halo that is a little misplaced, saying, "I am holy; you are not." You will never help your brother or sister that way. But when a moral issue is involved and your fellow believer refuses to obey the teaching of God's Word, then there must be a separation. You cannot follow the disobedient person and the Word of God at the same time. These exhortations are practical, but they are all linked with the command to be patiently waiting for the Lord's return. If we are doing this, we will be doing these things which are pleasing in the sight of God.

PAUL'S PRAYER FOR THEM (3:16–18)

3:16–18 Now may the Lord of peace himself give you peace at all times in every way. The Lord be with you all. I, Paul, write this greeting with my own hand. This is the sign of genuineness in every letter of mine; it is the way I write. The grace of our Lord Jesus Christ be with you all.

Paul began this chapter by commanding the Thessalonian believers to pray for him, and now he reciprocated and prayed for them. Prayer provides wonderful comradeship and fellowship. Paul prayed for three things: (1) that they would enjoy God's peace, (2) that they would have a sense of His presence, and (3) that God's grace would be their daily experience. The third petition is both a prayer and benediction. Consider these requests: God's peace that passes all understanding; His presence, never failing; and His grace, His attitude of love and favor toward us. Certainly of all people we are the most blessed. In spite of all our trials and troubles, when the Lord is on our side we have more than anyone else. Being a Christian in trial is far better than not being a Christian and having all the luxuries and comforts that the world can offer.

Paul considered it important that his readers recognize the genuineness of this letter as from him—that is, written by an apostle under the inspiration of the Holy Spirit. This makes all the difference in the world regarding the letter's authority and status as the Word of God. This would have been especially important and meaningful to the Thessalonians, who had been temporarily deceived by a forged letter supposedly from Paul (cf. 2:1–2). Therefore Paul authenticated this letter by taking the pen from his scribe and writing the benediction in his own handwriting (cf. 1 Cor. 16:21; Gal. 6:11; Col. 4:18).

As we conclude this study of 1 and 2 Thessalonians, may the prayer of the apostle Paul, given so long ago to these Christians, be ours. May the Lord's peace be our portion. May the consciousness of His presence be a daily, moment-by-moment experience. May "the grace of our Lord Jesus Christ be with you all."

NOTE

1. Warren W. Wiersbe, *The Bible Exposition Commentary: An Exposition of the New Testament*, vol. 2 (Wheaton, IL: Victor, 1989), 204.

 # Bibliography

Barnhouse, Donald Grey. *Thessalonians: An Expositional Commentary.* Grand Rapids: Zondervan, 1977.

Bruce, F. F. *1 and 2 Thessalonians.* Word Biblical Commentary Series, ed. Ralph P. Martin. Vol. 45. Waco: Word Books, 1982.

Constable, Thomas L. "First Thessalonians." *The Bible Knowledge Commentary.* Vol. 2, *New Testament.* Edited by John F. Walvoord and Roy B. Zuck. Wheaton, IL: Victor Books, 1983.

Hiebert, D. Edmond. *The Thessalonian Epistles.* Chicago: Moody Press, 1971.

Jackman, David. *The Authentic Church: A Study of the Letters to the Thessalonians.* Great Britain: Christian Focus, 1998.

MacArthur, John Jr. *1 & 2 Thessalonians.* Chicago: Moody Press, 2002.

Marshall, I. Howard. *1 and 2 Thessalonians.* The New Century Bible Commentary, ed. Matthew Black. Grand Rapids: Eerdmans, 1983.

Mayhue, Richard. *First and Second Thessalonians.* Focus on the Bible. Great Britain: Christian Focus, 1999.

Morris, Leon. *1 & 2 Thessalonians*, rev. ed. Tyndale New Testament Commentaries, ed. Leon Morris. Grand Rapids: Eerdmans, 1984.

Ryrie, Charles Caldwell. *First and Second Thessalonians.* Everyman's Bible Commentary. Chicago: Moody Press, 1959.

Stedman, Ray C. *Waiting for the Second Coming: Studies in Thessalonians.* Grand Rapids: Discovery House, 1990.

Stott, John R. W. *The Gospel and the End of Time: The Message of 1 & 2 Thessalonians.* Downers Grove, IL: InterVarsity, 1991.

Swindoll, Charles R. *Contagious Christianity: A Study of I Thessalonians.* Bible Study Guide. Anaheim, CA: Insight for Living, 1993.

Swindoll, Charles R. *Steadfast Christianity: A Study of Second Thessalonians.* Bible Study Guide. Anaheim, CA: Insight for Living, 1986.

Thomas, Robert L. *1 Thessalonians* and *2 Thessalonians.* The Expositor's Bible Commentary. Vol. 11. Edited by Frank E. Gaebelein and J. D. Douglas. Grand Rapids: Zondervan Publishing House, 1978.

Wiersbe, Warren. "1 Thessalonians" and "2 Thessalonians" in *The Bible Exposition Commentary.* Vol 2. Wheaton: Victor Books, 1989.

Subject Index

Boxes are indicated by b following the page numbers.

Scripture Index

OLD TESTAMENT

UPDATED CLASSICS
NOT TO BE MISSED

978-0-8024-1744-2

978-0-8024-7312-7

978-0-8024-0248-6

A renewed series of commentaries from respected evangelical theologian John F. Walvoord!

All of these books feature the great teaching of Dr. Walvoord but have been streamlined and refined, while using the English Standard Version (ESV). They also feature updated content from experts Charles Dyer and Mark Hitchcock. If you are looking for a trusted series of books to learn about Bible prophecy, look no further than the John Walvoord Prophecy Commentaries!

MOODY
Publishers™

From the Word to Life